MEZCAL
+
TEQUILA
COCKTAILS

MEZCAL + TEQUILA

COCKTAILS

Mixed drinks for the golden age of agave

ROBERT SIMONSON

Photographs by Lizzie Munro

TEN SPEED PRESS
California | New York

DEDICATED TO ASHER,
MARY KATE, AND RICHARD.

▰▰▰▰▰

GO TEAM.

MEZCAL COCKTAILS

TEQUILA COCKTAILS

MEZCAL + TEQUILA COCKTAILS

INTRODUCTION

Fifteen years ago, a book called "Mezcal and Tequila Cocktails" wouldn't have been published. Oh, "Tequila Cocktails" might have seen the light of day. But even that would have been a stretch once you got past the few widely known and consumed drinks, such as the margarita, paloma, and tequila sunrise. And then there would have been the question as to whether anyone would buy it. After all, for much of the twentieth century, tequila was known more for shots than mixing. You didn't savor it; you threw it back.

As for mezcal cocktails, well, there were none to speak of. Hell, in the United States market, there was almost no mezcal. And what mezcal there was—that forbidding bottle with the worm in it—wasn't very good and was little understood by the bartenders who poured it and the few drinkers who ordered it. If tequila was a dare you took up in a bar, and regretted the morning after, mezcal was a double-dog dare, a journey into the truly unknown.

Tequila's and mezcal's reputations today could not be more different. The spirits have enjoyed a complete turnaround in both status and popularity. In the 1920s, when Prohibition was in effect, Americans began traveling south of the border to drink agave spirits because they couldn't lay their hands on anything alcoholic at home. Today, Americans drink them out of preference. Consumers' eyes have been opened to the spirits' historical and artisanal heritage, and that they are the products of centuries of tradition and craftsmanship. Their newly elevated status reflects the endless agricultural variety of the hearty agave plant, from which both tequila and mezcal are derived, and their terroir, not to mention the inimitable touch of the *tequileros* and *mezcaleros* who create the liquors, many of whom are following family practices that go back generations. The distillates have finally joined other spirits commonly labeled with adjectives such as "elegant," "complex," and—that favorite term of marketers—"premium." In short, agave spirits have gone from shots to sipping; from the kind of hooch that Hollywood actors drink in disreputable cantinas in B pictures to the kind that Hollywood actors invest in and get rich off, in some cases making more money than they do from acting.

It's a Cinderella story unlike any in the drinks world, in which an age-old spirit has finally been recognized for the liquor royalty it always was. And, as with most spirits and cocktails that have gone from zero to sixty in popular favor these days, we can thank our ever-curious neighborhood mixologists for the change in public perception, as well as the journalists who cover their every move. Once the new breed of conscientious young bartenders were done blowing the dust off neglected spirits, like gin and rye and all sorts of underappreciated liqueurs and bitters, they turned their attentions to agave-based spirits. They wondered if tequila and mezcal maybe deserved to inhabit a better world of drinking, one that wasn't so reliant on lime wedges and salt and late-night bad decisions.

One of the first wonderers may have been Julio Bermejo. Bermejo is a San Franciscan whose dreams of a career in the diplomatic corps didn't pan out. Instead, in the 1980s, he found himself trapped behind the bar at his family's business, Tommy's Mexican Restaurant. There was a house margarita at Tommy's, just as there was at every Mexican restaurant. And, like the ones at most of those other places, it wasn't very good. Julio, making the best of his situation, decided to invent a better margarita. His first move was to get rid of the "mixto" tequila (a mix of agave spirit and neutral grain spirit) and use better-quality tequila made from 100 percent agave spirit. His second fix was to eighty-six the chemically laced sour mix and use

freshly squeezed lime juice in its place. The final step was the most radical: Bermejo removed the traditional curaçao from the recipe—the orange liqueur that technically made a margarita *a margarita*. (The name is Spanish for "Daisy," a daisy being an old category of cocktail that typically includes curaçao or grenadine.) He replaced it with agave syrup—not sugar, but syrup made from the same plant that produces tequila.

Bermejo's rationale behind all this was to place tequila, good tequila, on a pedestal so drinkers might better admire its fine character. He knew that was never going to a happen if he served cheap mixto smothered in sour mix and orange liqueur. The drink he served—the one that eventually became known and served the world over as Tommy's Margarita (page 119)—was essentially a tequila sour. But it was Tequila with a capital *T*.

Young bartenders took note. Soon, Tommy's Mexican Restaurant became one of the early agoras for thoughtful young mixologists looking to improve their lot and their cocktails. One of those bartenders was a South African named Jacques Bezuidenhout. He worked with Bermejo at the short-lived San Francisco agave bar Tres Agaves and there came up with La Perla, a daring mixture of reposado tequila, manzanilla sherry, and pear liqueur. The drink was revolutionary for 2005, ahead of its time. But its time was soon to come.

Bermejo's counterpart in Europe was a former high school teacher from Los Angeles named Tomas Estes. Estes found his place in the world selling Mexican food and tequila, first in Amsterdam and then in London, where he opened Café Pacifico in 1982. Estes kept a goodly selection of tequilas behind the bar. But, really, at that time, any selection of tequilas would have made an impression on Londoners and London bartenders, who knew little about the spirit. Noteworthy, too, were his margaritas, which used 100 percent agave tequila, good triple sec, and freshly squeezed lime juice. Even Dick Bradsell, then Britain's preeminent cocktail bartender, was impressed. Estes went on to a career as tequila evangelist, conducting seminars and classes and writing articles about his favorite spirit. Eventually, in 2008, he collaborated on his own brand, Tequila Ocho.

Another early player helping to move the needle in the agave renaissance was David Suro. Suro was born in the heart of tequila country, in Guadalajara. Marriage brought him to Philadelphia, where he got a job at a Mexican restaurant in the city's downtown. Dismayed by what passed for Mexican food and drink in the States, he bought out the owners in 1986 at the tender age of twenty-four and changed the name of the restaurant to Tequilas. The name made sense to him.

"*Tequila* means 'place of work,'" he said. "I found that very appropriate. I was going to be working my butt off for years, long days. But the name was a big challenge in 1986. People don't trust a place called Tequilas. They think there will be trouble. It was a battle with the community to try to tell them that there is nothing wrong with that name, that there is a lot of history and culture behind it."

That battle of perception became his cause. Every day, he labored to change the public's understanding of tequila. He fought against the clichés perpetuated by the big tequila companies—the silly, dissolute world of the shot glass; the salt; the lime; the kitschy pop hit "Tequila" by the Champs. "For us to walk through one thousand years of history in the relationship between man and plant and distill that into a drop of stereotypes, into a drop of nonsense," Suro continued, "I didn't want to do that."

Suro's advocacy over the decades has taken many forms, from Siembra Azul, his line of 100 percent agave tequilas, to the endless series of seminars he conducts, expanding consumer knowledge of agave spirits, to the many trips to Jalisco and Oaxaca he has hosted, introducing bartenders and other liquor professionals to the artisans and traditions behind the bottles they enjoy. He even created Siembra Valles Ancestral, his recent attempt at a tequila as it might have been made a century ago, before international success forever altered production methods.

Bermejo, Estes, and Suro were all advocates of enjoying agave spirits on their own. But the bartenders they were connecting with were members of the growing cocktail revival, which was, by the turn of the current century, beginning to gird the globe. These cocktail evangelists had other ideas. And so, as tequila and mezcal were rapidly being rediscovered by audiences the world over, the spirits were more

often than not found at the bottom of a cocktail glass, mingling with other friendly liquids.

✦✦✦✦✦

In New York City, around 2007, along a couple blocks of the East Village, tequila's and mezcal's fortunes—in a cocktail context, at least—were changed for good and forever. There, opening within months of each other, stood two new cocktail bars: Death & Co on East Sixth Street and PDT on St. Mark's Place. The former was run (if not owned) by bartender Phil Ward; the latter by bartender Jim Meehan. Ward possessed a preternatural ability to concoct new, yet simple, cocktail recipes with surprising frequency. By the time he got to Death & Co, he had created dozens of drinks. But it wasn't until he reached for a tequila bottle and a mezcal bottle that he found his true calling as one of the mixology world's Pied Pipers of agave. He plugged a little mezcal and a bit more reposado (that is, slightly aged) tequila into a standard old-fashioned template and came up with the Oaxaca Old-Fashioned (page 136). Like Julio Bermejo, he used agave syrup instead of sugar as the sweetener. The cocktail quickly became the breakout liquid star at Death & Co. Tequila old-fashioneds were not unheard of before 2007, but no old-fashioned featured mezcal, which lent an unfamiliar and exciting depth of flavor to the mix. (By 2019, the cocktail was so popular that Death & Co began selling Oaxaca Old-Fashioned T-shirts.)

The Oaxaca Old-Fashioned was the only mezcal recipe that Jim Meehan had heard of in 2008, when, two blocks north, at PDT, he took another old cocktail, the Moscow mule, and gave it the mezcal treatment, swapping out the usual vodka for the agave spirit. He kept the requisite lime juice and ginger beer, but, employing the old wine-world maxim "If it grows with it, it goes with it," he added passion fruit puree and cucumber slices and a pinch of ground chile. The result, in Meehan's words, was "strong, sweet, sour, smoky, vegetal, hot, and even a little floral." The Mezcal Mule (page 61) had legs as long as the Oaxaca Old-Fashioned. Today, countless bars and restaurants serve some sort of mezcal-based mule.

Both of those cocktails used mezcal made by the same company, Del Maguey, founded in 1995. There were a few good reasons for that. One, the mezcals that Del Maguey imported were of good quality and authentic provenance. More significantly, they were some of the *only* good mezcals then on the US market. Finally, they were the work of a man named Ron Cooper, without whose guidance most American bartenders would have remained in the dark about the true nature and history of mezcal.

Cooper wasn't a booze businessman. He was an artist who lived in Taos, New Mexico, and liked to visit Mexico. In 1990, during a months-long stay in the Mexican state of Oaxaca, where most mezcal is made, he became friendly with some of the family distillers who made mezcal with the old, traditional, painstaking method. Theirs were the sort of mezcals that never went very far beyond the villages where they were distilled. Cooper traveled down dusty country roads on his off days and befriended various mezcaleros, collecting dozens of samples of their mezcals along the way. He quickly became fascinated by the differences between the various distillates, which he ascribed to the wide variety of terroirs where the agaves were grown, as well as the different methods by which the plants were fermented and distilled.

In the years that followed, Cooper slowly entered the spirits business. He made it his personal mission to bring mezcal to the United States, where the spirit was dimly known and enjoyed no respect as an artisanal, ancestral elixir. Cooper viewed the different mezcals made at rustic distilleries (called *palenques*) in his own quirky way—as works of art, not unlike the art he himself created. His company coined the term "Single Village Mezcal" to communicate the idea of this individuality of expression. Mezcal wasn't a monolithic liquid, but a spirit bearing the imprints of the many different minds and hands who lovingly brought it into being.

He began his enterprise with mezcals from the villages Chichicapa and San Luis del Río. By 1998, he was importing four more varieties. Each was sold in a bright green bottle adorned by a colorful and simple drawing by his artist friend Ken Price. These distinctive bottles soon became a familiar sight to cocktail aficionados. Bartenders who embraced the brand, and mezcal in general, tended to carry all six types and placed them together, side by side, in a prominent place behind the bar, as if they were spiritous soldiers in the war of good taste. As a grouping, the eye-catching Del Maguey bottles were hard for the bar goer to miss.

Together, the Del Maguey varieties helped illustrate to the curious drinker the innate versatility of mezcal, a spirit that was then universally described as "smoky," but wasn't always. Del Maguey's mezcals were sometimes vegetal, floral, fruity, mineral, or salty, and many other things besides. Cooper probably did more to change mezcal's fortunes and reputation in the United States and the world than any other person.

In the 1990s, Cooper was greatly aided in this mission by Steve Olson, an industrious Iowan and Cooper's first big Stateside champion. Olson was then, as he is now, a charismatic roving wine, spirits, and cocktail consultant with a boundless and restless energy. (Picture a roadside revivalist who preaches about not the evils of drink, but its virtues.) Chefs and bartenders were largely ignorant of the characteristics, and even the basic makeup, of mezcal at that time. And certainly they were completely unfamiliar with Ron Cooper. But they all knew Olson, who became their connection to the unknown world of agave.

In 2009, Cooper began bringing bartenders down to Oaxaca to introduce them to mezcaleros and their world. Each was sent back with a bottle of mezcal to experiment with. And experiment they did. Cooper wasn't much for mixed drinks; he was a purist where mezcal was concerned and, like all spirit purists, viewed it as a sipping spirit, meant to be drunk on its own. His idea of a mezcal cocktail is the Mezcal Collins (page 51), which is nothing but 2 ounces of the spirit topped with soda water. But even he freely admits that, in the United States, cocktails became people's initiation into the spirit.

"Without the support of bartenders around the country and the world who were fond of our mezcal," wrote Cooper in his book *Finding Mezcal* (2018), "Del Maguey would not be what it is today. Cocktails have become one of the gateways to mezcal, and they continue to push the spirit into exciting new spaces."

By 2009, such aha moments as Phil Ward's and Jim Meehan's experiences with the Oaxaca Old-Fashioned and Mezcal Mule were becoming more common. New tequila and mezcal cocktails were popping up all over the map, quickly finding thirsty and adventurous new audiences. That year, Julian Cox, working at Rivera in Los Angeles, muddled lime wedges, red bell pepper, red Fresno chile, ginger syrup, lemon juice, and agave nectar to create the Barbacoa, a garden-fresh mezcal cocktail that took the city by storm. On the other side of the country, in New York, Maks Pazuniak, a bartender who has worked at Cure in New Orleans and several bars in New York City, came up with the Salt and Ash (page 138) when he was bartending at the Counting Room in Brooklyn. A split base of grapefruit-infused tequila and mezcal was combined with Lapsang souchong tea–infused sweet vermouth, lemon juice, agave syrup, maraschino liqueur, and Angostura and orange bitters. The Salt and Ash became his calling card.

In San Francisco, bartender Thad Vogler, then working with the restaurant Beretta, kept it simple, combining mezcal with lime juice and pineapple gum syrup (made by local company Small Hand Foods) for his Single Village Fix (page 79). Also paring down the ingredient list was Joaquín Simó. His drink Naked and Famous (page 69), at Death & Co, was a riff on Last Word, substituting mezcal for the usual gin, and adding Aperol, yellow Chartreuse, and lime juice. The drink wasn't a far cry from Phil Ward's own Division Bell, made of mezcal, Aperol, maraschino liqueur, and lime juice, which appeared on the first menu at Ward's bar Mayahuel, in New York City, and became nearly as well known as the Oaxaca Old-Fashioned.

Mayahuel was important. It was one of the first of a new breed of cocktail bar in the United States to focus specifically on agave spirits. There weren't just one or two tequila or mezcal cocktails on the menu—the entire menu was tequila and mezcal cocktails. In 2009, when Mayahuel opened, I, like most people, was an agave novice. I had tried Ward's Oaxaca Old-Fashioned and liked it, but I figured that was because I like old-fashioneds, not tequila and mezcal. A whole menu made up of such drinks struck me as perhaps too much of a

single thing. Those doubts were quieted, however, when, upon my first visit, I encountered one great drink after another; Division Bell, Stone Raft (jalapeño-infused tequila, mezcal, sherry, agave syrup, celery bitters), Pale Rider (jalapeño-infused tequila, sherry, cucumber, mint). Each one was a winner.

Within a few years, Mayahuel was no longer a lone outpost. "Mezcaleria" was now a familiar word to consumers, and every city seemed to have one. There was Pastry War in Houston, Las Perlas in Los Angeles, Espita Mezcaleria in Washington D.C., Ghost Donkey in Manhattan, Clavel Mezcaleria in Baltimore, La Reina in Santa Fe. Chicago, of all places, had so many mezcalerias that it was difficult to keep track. As the bars proliferated, so did the number of bartenders devoted to the juice. Journalists no longer had to turn to Ward or Cooper for quotes; there were agave experts aplenty. Most of them traveled to Mexico several times a year and knew the people who produced their favorite mezcals personally. They were a passionate group, fiercely protective of their favored spirit.

The mezcal renaissance spread quickly. By around 2017, you didn't even have to go to a mezcaleria to get your agave fix. Agave drinks were all over the place—at restaurants and bars and in hotels and resorts—because drinkers everywhere demanded them. And consumers were no longer willing to abide by the bartender's advice and suggested concoctions. They wanted tequila and mezcal *their* way, on their own terms; and their way was *every* way. Back in the '00s, a common order was, "I'd like that cocktail, but could you make it with vodka?" In the '10s, the new substitute spirit was mezcal. As Gary Crunkleton, who owns the Crunkleton bar in Chapel Hill, North Carolina, said, "I can remember when the spelling of mezcal was debatable. And now it is becoming the spirit of choice."

And, so, a Negroni, sure, but make it a mezcal Negroni, please. Daiquiri sounds good, but can I have mezcal instead of rum? Mezcal old-fashioneds, mezcal Manhattans, mezcal Last Words, mezcal Corpse Revivers, mezcal Aviations—you name it, they drank it. Even tequila had to take a back seat, as drinkers clamored from coast to coast for mezcal margaritas and mezcal palomas. But tequila also benefited greatly from mezcal's rise, as many of the new cocktails, like the Oaxaca Old-Fashioned, paired the two agave spirits. Mezcaleros and tequileros may not historically have had much communication with one another in Mexico, but that meant nothing to the bartenders up north. All that mattered was the two spirits got along in the glass. That rule eventually came to include other, more obscure agave spirits, like raicilla and bacanora.

In the beginning of the agave boom, the flavor pairings in cocktails got to be a bit monotonous, and even the most casual of observers caught on to the common kneejerk combinations. Jalapeño, sherry, grapefruit, ginger, pineapple, pear, lime juice—agave spirits have some best buds, to be sure, and liked to hang out with them a lot. But after a few years, bartenders' minds broadened, and they realized that tequila and mezcal—somewhat miraculously—could be teamed with almost anything. Orgeat, crème de cacao, crème de menthe, Old Tom gin, Irish whiskey, absinthe. It was all good. The spirits were suddenly the most versatile since gin.

If someone asked me to concisely explain the sudden popularity of agave spirits in the 2010s, I'd say that mezcal is this generation's single-malt Scotch. It answers to all the needs that single-malt Scotch did when it became the rage back in the 1990s. It is a very old spirit that seems new, simply because the world beyond Mexico has been relatively unexposed to it. It appeals as something authentic and artisanal, made by hand, and in relatively small amounts. It is expensive and answers to the current definition of luxury goods. And it is rough and smoky and edgy on the tongue, full of uncompromising flavors that are translated by our brain as "real." It is a spirit on hyperdrive, something tailor-made for the modern American palate's ever-growing need for more—more flavor, more sensation, a greater challenge.

The big difference between single-malt Scotch and mezcal is that mezcal mixes. The Scotch craze of the '90s produced no catalog of great modern cocktails. Blended Scotch mixes, a bit. But single-malt Scotch stands alone. Moreover, Scotch's fans don't really want it mixed. They are a sipping, savoring, somewhat sanctimonious crowd

who don't want anything, not even ice, touching their precious nectar. Mezcal lovers are sippers, too. But they're open to collaboration, to cocktails. And they're lucky, because agave likes to mingle.

This book is for them. Since tequila and, particularly, mezcal have stepped into the spotlight and become better known internationally, a number of books have been devoted to them. Because the spirits are not widely understood outside of their origin country, these books have taken pains to go into some depth about the history and culture of mezcal and tequila—how they are made; who makes them; the various varieties of agave species and growing regions; as well as delving into the various societal and environmental challenges that the industries now face. There is a bibliography at the back of this book for those keen to learn more about these subjects.

This book, meanwhile, is a recipe book, plain and simple, inspired by the many wonderful agave cocktails that I encountered in the growing number of agave bars that I have visited in my travels. It is filled with good and easy recipes so that the growing number of agave enthusiasts can enjoy agave spirits more often and in more varied ways.

The recipes that follow are some of the best the agave bars and agave wizards in the world have to offer, including a dozen or so that have achieved the status of modern classics. Most are easy to assemble. I've tried to keep the special syrups and infusions needed to a minimum. The few that require a bit more lifting are worth the effort, I promise you. The recipes are also very different from one another. Just as no two tequilas or mezcals taste alike, neither do any of these cocktails.

To aid you in finding the recipes, among the following sixty or so, that are most likely to please your established drinking preferences, I've included a handy chart on pages 153 through 157. Whether your regular drink is an old-fashioned, Manhattan, martini, daiquiri, or mai tai, it will point you in the right direction, agavewise.

WHAT ARE MEZCAL
AND TEQUILA, ANYWAY?:
A BRIEF PRIMER

You needn't know everything about the centuries-old history of agave spirits to enjoy them. But if you're going to drink them, you might as well become familiar with the basics. Tequila and mezcal are both distilled from the agave plant, a family of big, spiky succulents of various sizes and shapes that look like relatives of the cactus but are actually closer kin to the asparagus family. Agave plants are native to the southwestern United States, Mexico, and Central and South America. They take forever to grow, are great at storing up sugars, and have been converted into intoxicating beverages since forever.

Mezcal is historically the mother spirit, tequila being just one of her children—albeit the one that left the nest and made a lot of money and got its name in the papers. One used to be able to say, by way of easy definition, that all tequila is mezcal, but not all mezcal is tequila. That's still true from a Mother Nature point of view. However, recent laws in Mexico, passed to protect the definition of *mezcal*, have bestowed official recognition to just nine Mexican states (Durango, Guerrero, Guanajuato, Michoacán, Oaxaca, Puebla, San Luis Potosí, Tamaulipas, Zacatecas), none of which is Jalisco, the famous home of tequila. (Tequila can also be legally made in certain municipalities of Guanajuato, Michoacán, Nayarit, and Tamaulipas.) Therefore, tequila, *legally*, can no longer be called a mezcal. Tequila is tequila, and tequila only. But that's like saying Kleenex isn't facial tissue, it's just Kleenex. In broader historical terms, away from all the bureaucrats and lawyers and other busybodies, tequila is still a kind of mezcal.

Additionally, mezcal that has been made in Mexican states that don't enjoy the official designation of the government can no longer be lawfully called mezcal. Some have been forced (or have chosen, in defiance) to call their spirits *destilado de agave*. All this, too, is politically imposed nonsense.

Officially, there are different kinds of tequila and mezcal, which are reflected on the labels. Tequila, with its longer history of international marketing initiatives, comes in several types. Blanco ("white") is unaged and is bottled within sixty days of distillation. (You can rest blanco for up to fifty-nine days in wood or age for as long as you'd like in glass or stainless steel.) Reposado ("rested") is aged in oak anywhere from two months to a year. Añejo ("aged") is aged in oak for one to three years. Extra añejo (for those buyers who need their tequila to be as extra as possible) is aged for three years or more. Mixto, as was mentioned earlier, is a mixture of 51 percent blue agave and 49 percent who-knows-what. That's all you need to know. Avoid it.

Mezcal isn't as focused on aging as tequila. Some brands have started to put out aged products, but the bulk is released right off the still. There are, however, other fairly recent legal definitions that address matters other than age, including roasting (the agave hearts, or *piñas*), fermentation, and distilling. "Mezcal" is the broadest category. It can be cooked in an underground earthen pit, a masonry oven, autoclave, or diffuser. The agave hearts can be milled any old way, by hand or machine; fermented in wooden, masonry, or stainless-steel tanks; and distilled in pot or column stills. As you can see, the bar is set pretty low to meet this certification. "Mezcal artisanal" insists on roasting in earthen pits or masonry ovens only; milling by hand or with a molino (a large stone wheel called a "tahona" in tequila production), crusher, or shredder; fermentation in clay pots, stone, wood, or animal skins; and distilled over a direct fire in copper or clay stills, with agave fibers included. The most finicky level is "mezcal ancestral," which allows only earthen pits; milling by hand, molino, or mills; wood, stone, clay, and animal-skin fermentation; and direct-fire, clay-pot stills.

These rules, as you might expect, are imperfect and insufficiently nuanced to be able to contain the age-old, sprawling cultural spectrum of mezcal and mezcaleros. It's a volleyball net trying to capture an entire monarch migration. It's also a recipe for chicanery, injustice, corruption, and confusion. My advice is, when shopping for mezcal, don't rely on government labels to do the thinking for you. Sound out trusted liquor stores and bars and bartenders about the true provenance of any given mezcal and buy accordingly.

The meaningful differences in mezcal type boil down to three things: what agave species were used, where they were grown, and who distilled them.

Only one kind of agave, Blue Weber, can be used to make tequila, while dozens are allowed by law to be used in making mezcal. But today, outside of Mexico, when mixing cocktails with mezcal, you're really going be dealing with just a handful of agave varieties, and one in particular. The majority of mezcals currently on the shelves are made from espadín, the most commonly grown agave variety in Oaxaca. Espadín grows to maturity in roughly eight years—lightning speed in comparison to most agave species, which can take up to thirty years to ripen. It is widely farmed but also grows wild. The widespread use of espadín in mezcal production, however, doesn't mean different brands and bottles are going to taste like the same old, same old. A tasting of a few espadín mezcals side by side at your local mezcaleria will quickly dispel that notion.

Still, for the above reasons, and for the purposes of this book, espadín is the main type of mezcal you need to know and have in your home bar. Nearly all of the mezcal cocktails in this book called for mezcal espadín of some brand or other, typically the ubiquitous Vida brand by the trailblazing company Del Maguey.

There is a good reason for this. Vida is one of the more affordable of the baseline espadín mezcals out there and therefore makes economic sense in a bartender's well, where using a more expensive (and perhaps better) mezcal would price a drink off the menu. (Many of the most elite mezcal bottlings are too rare or expensive to use in cocktails; they are meant for fat wallets and sipping neat.) Using Vida also makes practical sense because it is one of the most widely available of mezcal brands. (Del Maguey's mezcals are the most widely distributed globally.) There's nothing more frustrating than wanting to make a recipe in a cocktail book and then finding that your local liquor stores do not carry the specific brand recommended for the drink. If your liquor store carries only one mezcal, chances are it is Vida.

And that's okay. It is not a bad, or boring, thing to reach for Vida when making a cocktail that simply calls for mezcal. The opinionated mezcal maven may not regard it as the most exciting expression of the spirit, but it is a worthy and durable item and, in broad terms, does what a mezcal is supposed to do in a cocktail. Vida is currently performing the role taken in the past by other benchmark liquors. Famous Grouse may not be the ultimate blended Scotch out there, just as Evan Williams isn't the best bourbon on the market or Old Overholt the best rye whiskey. But they do just fine when working inside the confines of a Rob Roy or Manhattan or old-fashioned. Every spirit category needs a go-to, available, affordable, and mixable brand. At this moment in time, mezcal has Vida.

As far as Tequila goes, there are a vast variety of affordable 100 percent agave brands on the market, so the consumer is afforded more choice within a modest price range. Tapatio, a long-standing estate-grown brand, is a favorite of mine, both the blanco and reposado. If you can find the overproof version, bottled at 55% ABV, buy it. It's packed with flavor. El Tesoro and Ocho, made at the same Highlands distillery as Tapatio, and Siembra Valles, a brand imported by David Suro, are also excellent.

EQUIPMENT

I would recommend investing in each of the items listed here. Presentation and precision go a long way toward making a good cocktail. It needn't cost you much, maybe fifty dollars tops if you shop wisely. And the outlay will pay dividends for years to come.

If you want to get particular, and don't mind spending a little extra, I recommend the bar equipment put out by Cocktail Kingdom (www.cocktailkingdom.com) and Modern Mixologist (www.themodernmixologist.com). Full disclosure: Cocktail Kingdom and I have collaborated on a set of old-fashioned glasses. If you want to have a little fun shopping, antique and vintage shops, as well as yard sales and garage sales, are good sources for old cocktail glasses and coupes of various designs and styles.

Barspoon. A long barspoon (approximately 11 inches) is the preferred tool for stirring drinks. It holds a scant ¼ ounce when used for measuring.

Boston shaker. This two-piece shaker, composed of a standard mixing glass and a metal mixing tin, is suitable for both stirred drinks (for which you only need the mixing glass) and shaken drinks (for which you require both parts).

Cocktail strainer. Julep strainers, which have a perforated bowl, are for drinks made solely of spirits. However, a Hawthorne strainer, which is lined with a coiled spring for catching citrus pulp, will do the job as well.

Glassware. The various drinks that follow all call for a cocktail or a coupe glass (5 to 6 ounces), an old-fashioned or rocks glass (4 to 10 ounces), or a collins glass (10 to 14 ounces). Keep your glasses chilled, for at least 15 minutes, and do not remove them from the freezer until ready to use. If you forgot to prechill the glasses, a quick fix is to fill the glasses with ice and let them chill while you prepare the cocktails.

Jigger. Most jiggers have a dual-measure design. Typically, they measure either 1 ounce on one end and ½ ounce on the other, or 1½ ounces and ¾ ounce. Modern Mixologist makes a very versatile double jigger: one end has a 1½-ounce capacity, and the other has a 1-ounce capacity.

Muddler. A muddler is required for certain drinks that require you to mash up fruits, vegetables, herbs, or sugar cubes at the bottom of a mixing glass or serving glass. Old-fashioned wooden specimens work best.

Standard mixing glass. A pint glass can do in a pinch if you don't have a dedicated mixing glass. I prefer mixing glasses to cocktail tins, for the simple reason that you can see inside glass and keep track of how much you are diluting your drink. Many barware companies sell beautiful cut-glass mixing glasses. Naturally, these are more expensive than a standard pint glass, but they are a beautiful addition to any home bar and add an elegance to the drink-building ritual.

Trays or molds for large ice cubes. A large ice cube makes a big difference, both aesthetically and tastewise, in some stirred sipping drinks, such as variations on the old-fashioned and negroni. Molds for these sorts of cubes, typically 1½ or 2 inches, are now widely available, both online and in stores.

INGREDIENTS

The cocktail renaissance has spurred an increase in the production and availability of quality spirits, liqueurs, and bitters. Most cities now contain one or two well-curated liquor shops that can satisfy a home mixologist's every spirituous need.

Bitters. A dash is whatever comes out of a bottle of bitters when you upend it with a swift flick of the wrist. Be careful though: some bitters bottles dispense more quickly than others. Angostura aromatic bitters is the most famous brand of bitters and a product you must have in your arsenal. Second most important are orange bitters. In the past decade, the market has become flooded with orange bitters. In addition, you will need chocolate or mole bitters, which are often used to enhance agave cocktails. Bittermens is a good brand.

Garnishes. Garnishes are important. Just as much as bitters, they form a vital part of the cocktail. If you don't have lemons, olives, cherries, or cocktail onions on hand, don't make the drink.

Be sure your lemons, limes, oranges, and grapefruit are fresh and firm, with plenty of skin from which to carve your twists. Wash all fruit before using them; they may be covered with residual pesticides and other chemicals. To make a twist, use a vegetable peeler (a simple Y-shaped peeler will do) and try to cut away just the zest, leaving behind as much of the bitter white pith as possible. Express, or twist, the garnish over the surface of the drink to release the citrus oils, then slip it into the drink or hang it over the rim of the glass. Don't rub the twist along the rim, as it can leave a bitter taste, which will inform your every sip.

I recommend making cocktail cherries and onions from scratch, rather than buying a jar at the store. There are many recipes for brandied cherries and homemade cocktail onions to be found on the internet. It is worth the effort and will greatly improve your drinks. For cherries, use sour cherries, which have a short season during the summer, not the ubiquitous sweet variety.

Ice. I cannot emphasize enough the importance of using good ice when mixing these drinks. Keep your ice fresh. If ice has been sitting in your freezer for more than a couple of days, do not use it in a drink. Throw it out and make a fresh batch. Old ice has absorbed other flavors lurking in your freezer. Also, if your local tap water is not of sterling quality, I recommend using filtered or bottled water for your ice.

When making any of these drinks, do not be stingy with the ice. Fill your mixing glass nearly to the rim. Cocktails should be as cold as possible. Note: "Stir until chilled" usually means stirring for about 30 seconds. Where shaking is called for, shake vigorously for 15 seconds.

MEZCAL
COCKTAILS

BLACK CAT

NICK JARRETT, CLOVER CLUB, BROOKLYN (2010)

One of the more successful and long-lived modern mezcal cocktail classics is the Black Cat, Jarrett's riff on a reverse Martinez. "I've always preferred splitting the Old Tom gin between an older style, dry and lightly oaked, with the (relatively) newer sweet and mild style," said Jarrett. "I added in an equal part of Chichicapa mezcal for depth and smoke, then split the vermouth between Punt e Mes and amontillado sherry. The amontillado works well with grapefruit, and the Punt e Mes fills in for the bitters component. I took out the maraschino liqueur and replaced it with a grapefruit disk lightly muddled in a little bit of sirop du canne to get a little bit more bitterness and the grapefruit oils." The name owes to the fact that the drink hit the Clover Club menu around Halloween.

1 grapefruit disk

Scant 1 teaspoon sugarcane syrup

1 ounce Del Maguey Chichicapa or Vida mezcal

½ ounce Ransom Old Tom gin

½ ounce Hayman's Old Tom gin

½ ounce Punt e Mes

½ ounce Lustau amontillado sherry

Grapefruit twist for garnish

Muddle the grapefruit disk in the sugarcane syrup in the bottom of a mixing glass. Fill with ice and add the remaining ingredients. Stir until chilled, about 30 seconds. Fine strain into a chilled coupe. Express the grapefruit twist over the surface and drop it into the drink.

COCOA SMOKE

M. CARRIE ALLAN, *THE WASHINGTON POST* (2016)

Carrie Allan is the spirits and cocktail columnist for the *Washington Post* and one of the best writers covering the cocktail beat. She does a lot of R and D work in preparation for her columns, and occasionally an original drink comes out of the process. (Hey, if today's bartenders are going to insist on writing cocktail books, it's only fair that cocktail journalists be allowed to invent drinks.) This recipe accompanied a 2016 column. "The power trio of chocolate, the grassy smoke of mezcal, and ancho chile pepper liqueur makes for a heady, sexy sip," wrote Allan. The name of the drink says it all.

1½ ounces mezcal

½ ounce crème de cacao, preferably Tempus Fugit

½ ounce ancho chile liqueur

3 dashes chocolate bitters

Orange twist for garnish

Combine the ingredients, except the garnish, in a mixing glass three-quarters filled with ice. Stir until chilled, about 30 seconds. Strain into a chilled coupe. Express the orange twist over the surface and drop it into the drink.

DADOS

CAITLIN LAMAN, LICORERÍA LIMANTOUR,
MEXICO CITY (2016)

Some cocktails are more personal than others. Tasting this unusual sipper, you get the feeling that the bartender was in a particular mood and thinking particular thoughts when she came up with the unusual combination. This drink is a good illustration of how important the choice of mezcal can be in a cocktail. It will not taste the same with another mezcal. Though the French liqueur Suze can be quite the flavor bully, with its strong sweet-bitter gentian note, the La Luna mezcal overpowers it and commands the glass. The cocktail is basically a slightly adorned celebration of that particular mezcal. The twists of lemon and orange are essential.

1½ ounces La Luna mezcal

½ ounce Suze

Scant ¼ ounce Giffard crème de pamplemousse

2 dashes Angostura bitters

Lemon twist for garnish

Orange twist for garnish

Combine the ingredients, except the garnishes, in a mixing glass three-quarters filled with ice. Stir until chilled, about 30 seconds. Strain into a rocks glass filled with ice. Express the lemon and orange twists over the surface and drop them into the drink.

ELEGANTE

ROBERT SIMONSON, BROOKLYN (2020)

This is my simple twist on the Debonair, a 1993 drink by the late cocktail writer Gary Regan. His drink called for single malt Scotch. Mezcal, which is just as forthright at Scotch, works perfectly in the format. Make sure you use a firm lemon, whose peel will release plenty of oils.

2½ ounces mezcal
1 ounce ginger liqueur
Lemon twist for garnish

Combine the ingredients, except the garnish, in a mixing glass three-quarters filled with ice. Stir until chilled, about 30 seconds. Strain into a chilled coupe. Express the lemon twist over the surface and drop it into the drink.

FIRMIN'S FOLLY

DYLAN O'BRIEN, PRIZEFIGHTER,
EMERYVILLE, CALIFORNIA (2019)

This cocktail presents a nice, clean way to enjoy mezcal. The recipe is unmistakably in the martini family, and provides a platform for the spirit in the same way a martini does for gin. A touch of banana liqueur is welcome; it rounds out the drink and cuts back on its austerity. Prizefighter uses Del Maguey Vida mezcal here, but I've made it with a few others and found they work well; each delivers a slightly different drink, just as using a different gin will get you a different martini. Vermouth-wise, Prizefighter uses Carpano dry. And for the banana liqueur, there is no debate. There are few that match Tempus Fugit in flavor and complexity. The name of the drink is taken from the protagonist of Malcolm Lowry's novel *Under the Volcano* (1947), said O'Brien, "because it struck me as the kind of thing a British alcoholic might have drunk in the '40s while whiling away the day."

1½ ounces mezcal

¾ ounce dry vermouth

¼ ounce Tempus Fugit
crème de banane

2 dashes chocolate
or mole bitters

Combine the ingredients in a mixing glass three-quarters filled with ice. Stir until chilled, about 30 seconds. Strain into a chilled coupe. (No garnish.)

GUILLOTINE

FRANKY MARSHALL, LE BOUDOIR,
BROOKLYN (2015)

The original idea for this cocktail materialized after a guest requested a "similar but different" mezcal cocktail to the one just enjoyed. "For that one I used mezcal, Scotch, mint, lemon, and ginger. Then, when putting cocktails together for a menu I was working on, I decided to turn it into a stirred drink," Marshall said. "The Scotch-honey-banana were a given, but I hadn't realized how well banana worked with the mezcal, not to mention the mezcal-Scotch combination. The Guillotine became one of our best sellers, and was once referred to as 'a most elegant kick to the face.'" The unusual combination of the mezcal, Scotch, and banana liqueur lends this simple recipe an exotic feel that verges on decadent. It will steady your mind and nail you to your seat on the first sip, even if it doesn't quite detach your head from your body. Make it a nightcap.

1 ounce Illegal mezcal joven

¾ ounce Compass Box Great
King Street blended Scotch

¼ ounce Giffard Banane
du Brésil liqueur

¼ ounce honey syrup
(1:1 honey to water)

Lemon twist for garnish

Combine the ingredients, except the garnish, in a mixing glass three-quarters filled with ice. Stir until chilled, about 30 seconds. Strain into a snifter over one large ice cube. Express the lemon twist over the surface and drop it into the drink.

GUN METAL BLUE

NICK BENNETT, PORCHLIGHT, NEW YORK CITY (2015)

This drink was an instant hit, and an Instagram sensation, when Danny Meyer's first-ever bar, Porchlight, opened in 2015. It came along when both mezcal drinks and blue cocktails were enjoying a moment. The vibrant color caught drinkers' attention, but the flavor of this deceptively simple sour kept them coming back for more.

1½ ounces Del Maguey Vida mezcal

½ ounce blue curaçao

¼ ounce peach brandy

¾ ounce freshly squeezed lime juice

¼ ounce Cinnamon Syrup (page 144)

Orange peel coin for garnish

Combine the ingredients, except the garnish, in a cocktail shaker filled with ice. Shake until chilled, about 15 seconds. Strain into a chilled coupe. Express the orange peel coin over the drink and float it on the surface.

JOHANN GOES TO MEXICO

JOSEY PACKARD, DRINK, BOSTON (2010)

This cocktail, invented at the Boston cocktail bar Drink, is a mezcal riff on the Trinidad Sour, a modern cocktail classic that, improbably, calls for 1½ ounces of Angostura bitters, an ingredient typically deployed in small dashes as an accent. In Packard's version, only ½ ounce is called for. The lesser amount allows the mezcal's flavors to shine through.

1½ ounces mezcal, preferably Del Maguey Vida

½ ounce freshly squeezed lemon juice

½ ounce demerara syrup (1:1 demerara sugar to water)

½ ounce Angostura bitters

Combine the ingredients in a cocktail shaker filled with ice. Shake until chilled, about 15 seconds. Double strain into a chilled coupe. (No garnish.)

THE LAST MECHANICAL ART

MAKS PAZUNIAK, CURE, NEW ORLEANS (2011)

Back in 2009, two anarchy-inclined young bartenders named Kirk Estopinal and Maks Pazuniak, feeling their oats at a New Orleans cocktail bar called Cure, put together a thin, limited-edition manifesto called *Rogue Cocktails* and handed it to anyone who would take it. This was followed up one year later by *Beta Cocktails.* In both books, the duo, aided by some fellow travelers, attempted to blow up the mixology status quo with a few dozen crazy-looking drinks made up of ingredients that one wouldn't think would go well together. The books went on to become two of the more influential cocktail manuals in history, greatly furthering the fortunes of bitters and amari and other oddball ingredients in the cocktail world. As the authors were on the lookout for anything that wasn't the same old, same old, it's only natural that a few mezcal recipes landed in those pages. In this simple construct, Pazuniak reached for four bruising liquids, none of which pulls any punches. It's a dark, deep cocktail, and I'm not sure which ingredient wins. It's something to ponder while drinking it.

¾ ounce Del Maguey
Chichicapa mezcal

¾ ounce Cynar

¾ ounce Punt e Mes

¾ ounce Campari

Orange twist for garnish

Combine the ingredients, except the garnish, in a mixing glass three-quarters filled with ice. Stir until chilled, about 30 seconds. Strain into a chilled coupe. Express the orange twist over the surface and drop it into the drink.

MARTINA

MILES CRETTIEN AND GABRIEL WEINSTOCK,
LIS BAR, KINGSTON, NEW YORK (2019)

This is about as close as a mezcal drinker is going to get to drinking a Gibson. The mezcal base of this drink is given a tang and snap both by the olive brine and raicilla, a lesser-known agave spirit.

1½ ounces mezcal

½ ounce raicilla tabernas

¼ ounce cocktail onion brine

4 dashes celery bitters

Cocktail onion for garnish

Combine the ingredients, except the garnish, in a mixing glass three-quarters filled with ice. Stir until chilled, about 30 seconds. Strain into a chilled coupe. Garnish with the cocktail onion.

MAXIMILLIAN AFFAIR

MISTY KALKOFEN, GREEN STREET,
BOSTON (2008)

Boston-based bartender Misty Kalkofen was one of the early masters of mezcal cocktails and eventually became a brand ambassador for the Del Maguey mezcal line. This is an early invention of hers, created the night that Ron Cooper, the founder of Del Maguey, walked into Green Street, where she was working at the time. It's a simple drink with a complex outcome, tying in aspects of the Negroni, Manhattan, and sour.

1 ounce mezcal

1 ounce St-Germain
elderflower liqueur

½ ounce Punt e Mes

¼ ounce freshly squeezed
lemon juice

Lemon twist for garnish

Combine the ingredients, except the garnish, in a cocktail shaker filled with ice. Shake until chilled, about 15 seconds. Strain into a chilled coupe. Express the lemon twist over the surface and drop it into the drink.

MEZCAL COCKTAIL

THAD VOGLER, BAR AGRICOLE,
SAN FRANCISCO (2010)

The menus at the bars of Thad Vogler, an influential force in San Francisco drinking, are filled with simple drinks. There are reasons. One, Vogler is such a stickler for authenticity that his back bar features very few bottles. Two, he believes perfecting and mastering old cocktails is a far worthier pursuit than trying to invent new ones, and an approach that is more likely to result in a drink that is actually good. This recipe is the simplest in this book. It is a fifty-fifty mezcal Manhattan, basically, albeit with orange bitters and an orange twist to complement the base spirit. Use a mezcal made from the espadín agave varietal.

1 ounce mezcal, preferably an espadín mezcal joven

1 ounce sweet vermouth

3 dashes orange bitters

Orange twist for garnish

Combine the ingredients, except the garnish, in a mixing glass three-quarters filled with ice. Stir until chilled, about 30 seconds. Strain into a rocks glass over one large ice cube. Express the orange twist over the surface and drop it into the drink.

MEZCAL COLLINS

RON COOPER

This simple recipe illustrates Cooper's respect for mezcal as a spirit. A dose of soda water is as far as he'll go in an attempt to mix the spirit. He specifies a particular expression in the Del Maguey line, a fruity one grown in a high-altitude, tropical area in southern Oaxaca, but really any of Cooper's mezcals work in this format.

2 ounces Del Maguey Santo Domingo Albarradas mezcal

Soda water to top

Pour the mezcal into a collins glass filled with ice. Top with soda. (No garnish.)

MEZCAL
CORPSE REVIVER

CHARLES CERANKOSKY,
ROCHESTER, NEW YORK (2017)

Charles Cerankosky, a bar owner in Rochester, New York, has fielded plenty of creative mezcal-sub orders in his day. One of the most unusual requests was to switch out gin for mezcal in a Corpse Reviver, a sour that dates back a century. This twist is not a natural fit, so Cerankosky replaced the usual lemon juice with a mix of lime and grapefruit juice to better complement the mezcal. With all that's going on in this drink, the mezcal almost gets lost in the mix, if that's possible. Still, that smoke lingers in the back, and the panoply of flavors is intriguing enough to lure you back for another sip.

1 barspoon absinthe,
preferably St. George verte

1 ounce Cocchi Americano

¾ ounce mezcal,
preferably El Buho

¾ ounce curaçao,
preferably Pierre Ferrand dry

½ ounce freshly squeezed
grapefruit juice

¼ ounce freshly squeezed
lime juice

Coat the inside of a chilled coupe with absinthe, and discard the excess. Combine the Cocchi Americano, mezcal, curaçao, and both juices in a cocktail shaker filled with ice. Shake until chilled, about 15 seconds. Strain into the prepared coupe. (No garnish.)

MEZCALETTI

RICHARD BOCCATO, DUTCH KILLS, QUEENS (2015)

The ingredients of this drink are telegraphed by the name: mezcal and Amaro Meletti, built in a rocks glass filled with ice. Strong, nutty, and buttery, it has a surprising amount of depth for such a simple mixture. The cocktail made its debut at Dutch Kills, a Sasha Petraske bar now run by Richard Boccato that was the first serious cocktail den in the New York borough of Queens. It has since been served at Bar Clacson, Boccato's bar in Los Angeles.

1 ounce mezcal
1 ounce Amaro Meletti
2 dashes orange bitters
Lemon twist for garnish

Put a large ice cube in a chilled rocks glass and pour the liquid ingredients over the ice cube. Stir until chilled, about 15 seconds. Express the lemon twist over the surface and drop it into the drink.

MEZCALEXANDER

ROBERT SIMONSON, BROOKLYN (2020)

The Alexander, a classic cream drink, is a very adaptable cocktail. While it was originally made with gin, it achieved wide popularity as the Brandy Alexander. Mezcal, being a natural companion to chocolate flavors, works just as well.

2 ounces mezcal

1 ounce cream

1 ounce Tempus Fugit crème de cacao

Ground nutmeg for garnish

Combine the ingredients, except the garnish, in a cocktail shaker. Shake briefly without ice, about 5 seconds. Add ice, then shake until chilled, about 15 seconds more. Strain into a chilled coupe. Dust the surface with nutmeg.

MEZCAL FIX

The fix is basically a sour, but served over crushed ice. It's a small difference, but the change has a big impact. Few drinks are as likeable and refreshing as a fix, and this mezcal version is no exception. The rich simple syrup is critical for lending the cocktail some body. There's no need to shake the ingredients with ice; the drink will receive plenty of chilling and dilution once it hits that mountain of ice.

2 ounces mezcal

¾ ounce rich simple syrup
(2:1 sugar to water)

¾ ounce freshly squeezed
lime juice

Combine the ingredients in a cocktail shaker. Shake briefly without ice, for about 5 seconds. Strain into an old-fashioned glass filled with crushed ice. (No garnish.)

MEZCAL MARGARITA

PHIL WARD, MAYAHUEL, NEW YORK CITY (2009)

You can't have a mezcal cocktail book without a recipe for a mezcal margarita, the common mezcal-swap drink called for in bars today. Often, customers just ask for a "spicy margarita," but a mezcal margarita is what they mean. This recipe comes from a very sound source: Mayahuel, the first important agave craft cocktail bar in New York City.

Salt to rim the glass

2 ounces Del Maguey Vida mezcal

1 ounce Cointreau

¾ ounce freshly squeezed lime juice

Lime wedge for garnish

Half-rim a chilled rocks glass with salt and fill with a few large ice cubes. Combine the remaining ingredients, except the garnish, in a cocktail shaker filled with ice. Shake until chilled, about 15 seconds. Strain over the ice into the prepared rocks glass. Garnish with the lime wedge.

MEZCAL MULE

JIM MEEHAN, PDT, NEW YORK CITY (2008)

Mezcal Mules—Moscow Mules that call for mezcal instead of vodka—
are commonplace today. But they weren't when Jim Meehan came up
with this recipe at his famous New York speakeasy, PDT, in 2008.
"I was intrigued with how spirits (peated whisky or mezcal) could be
used to impart a smoky quality to cocktails," said Meehan. "There's an
old maxim in the wine world that 'if it grows with it, it goes with it.'
I brought this concept into the development process. Passion fruit is
common in Mexico, and has a heady aroma reminiscent of the natural,
open-vat fermentation of many mezcals. Cucumber, also common
there, reinforces the vegetal character of the spirit, while the lime and
ginger add acidity and earthiness, respectively. A pinch of Mexican
chile, which is commonly added to slices of jicama and oranges, served
as snacks in mezcalerias, adds heat and more earth." The result is
strong, sweet, sour, smoky, vegetal, hot, and even a little floral, and
has inspired many similar drinks.

3 cucumber slices,
plus 1 for garnish

½ ounce agave syrup
(1:1 agave nectar to water)

1½ ounces Del Maguey
Vida mezcal

1 ounce Ginger Wort
(page 145)

¾ ounce freshly squeezed
lime juice

¾ ounce Boiron
passion fruit puree

Candied ginger for garnish

Ground chile for garnish

Muddle the 3 cucumber slices and agave
syrup in the bottom of a mixing glass, then
add the remaining ingredients, except the
garnishes. Shake with ice and then fine strain
into a chilled double old-fashioned glass filled
with ice. Garnish with the piece of candied
ginger joined to a slice of cucumber on a pick
and add a sprinkle of ground chile (a salt
shaker works well for this).

MEZCAL NEGRONI

Among modern mezcal cocktails, there are perhaps more Negroni riffs than anything else. Like gin, the usual spirit in a Negroni, mezcal can stand up to the strong flavor personalities of vermouth and Campari. Many people like to increase the measure of mezcal in this drink to 1½ ounces, but I prefer the classic ratio of equal parts.

1 ounce mezcal
1 ounce sweet vermouth
1 ounce Campari
Orange twist for garnish

Combine the ingredients, except the garnish, in a mixing glass three-quarters filled with ice. Stir until chilled, about 30 seconds. Strain into a chilled rocks glass over one large ice cube. Express the orange twist over the surface and drop it into the drink.

MEZCAL SOUR

The simple sour is an extremely old and versatile cocktail template. The whiskey sour, gin sour, and daiquiri are just three popular examples of the genre. It was only natural that once mezcal arrived in cocktail bars, it would be given a spin on the formula. No surprise: it works beautifully.

2 ounces mezcal

1 ounce simple syrup
(1:1 sugar to water)

¾ ounce freshly squeezed
lemon juice

Combine the ingredients in a cocktail shaker filled with ice. Shake until chilled, about 15 seconds. Strain into a chilled coupe. (No garnish.)

MEZCALERO

Late bartender John Lermayer was a force in the Miami cocktail bar scene, where he opened his bar, Sweet Liberty. He created this Negroni variation following a trip to Oaxaca. Like other bartenders, he discovered that mezcal and Aperol, the Italian aperitif, were natural friends. The cocktail appeared on the bar's opening menu and is still there.

1 ounce Del Maguey
Vida mezcal

1 ounce Aperol

1 ounce blanc vermouth

Large grapefruit twist
for garnish

Combine the ingredients, except the garnish, in a mixing glass three-quarters filled with ice. Stir until chilled, about 30 seconds. Strain into an old-fashioned glass over one large ice cube. Express the grapefruit twist over the surface and drop it into the drink.

MEZCAPOLITAN

RYAN DEROSA, MUCHA LUCHA, MILWAUKEE (2018)

Mucha Lucha was Milwaukee's first mezcal bar. It opened in 2018, located in the basement space underneath the bar of the Hotel Madrid. This drink is DeRosa's approximation of a mezcal cosmopolitan. It comes remarkably close to the experience of the 1990s bar staple.

1¼ ounces Montelobos mezcal

½ ounce Hibiscus Grenadine (page 146)

½ ounce Pierre Ferrand dry curaçao

¾ ounce freshly squeezed lime juice

⅓ ounce cranberry cocktail

Lime wheel for garnish

Combine the ingredients, except the garnish, in a cocktail shaker filled with ice. Shake until chilled, about 15 seconds. Strain into a chilled coupe. Garnish with the lime wheel.

NAKED AND FAMOUS

JOAQUÍN SIMÓ, DEATH & CO, NEW YORK CITY (2011)

This equally proportioned drink has appeared on menus from Paris to Portland since it made its debut at Death & Co in New York. Like so many new cocktails from the late '00s, it's in the Last Word wheelhouse, with a nod to another modern classic, the Paper Plane.

¾ ounce mezcal

¾ ounce Aperol

¾ ounce yellow Chartreuse

¾ ounce freshly squeezed lime juice

Lime wedge for garnish

Combine the ingredients, except the garnish, in a cocktail shaker filled with ice. Shake until chilled, about 15 seconds. Strain into a chilled coupe. Garnish with the lime wedge.

PERFECT PEAR

MONY BUNNI, CHICAGO (2019)

Pear and mezcal are natural partners, as this tart-sweet, refreshing cocktail illustrates. The St. George spiced pear liqueur has a unique flavor—just as the name indicates, it tastes of pears and baking spices—and is required here; no other pear liqueur will do.

1½ ounces mezcal, preferably Cruz de Fuego Espadín

¾ ounce St. George spiced pear liqueur

¾ ounce freshly squeezed lemon juice

½ ounce Spiced Demerara Syrup (page 151)

2 dashes Bitter Truth aromatic bitters

1 whole star anise for garnish

Combine the ingredients, except the garnish, in a cocktail shaker filled with ice. Shake until chilled, about 15 seconds. Fine strain into chilled coupe. Garnish with the star anise, floated on the drink's surface.

POLAR BEAR

BON VIVANTS, TRICK DOG, SAN FRANCISCO (2013)

This riff on a stinger was a standout on the first menu of Trick Dog, one of San Francisco's leading cocktail bars. It was also one of the earliest mezcal cocktails to illustrate all the various and wonderful roles mezcal could play in a glass. Mezcal and crème de menthe are not, after all, what would strike one as a natural match. Bon Vivant's Josh Harris believes the angelica tincture adds something important to the flavor of the drink. But if you don't have the patience, or access to angelica root, a couple dashes of celery bitters will do the trick. Though the drink contains no citrus, dairy, or egg, its creators insist it should be shaken.

1½ ounces Mezcal Union

¾ ounce Dolin blanc vermouth

½ ounce Tempus Fugit crème de menthe

6 drops Angelica Tincture (page 143)

Combine the ingredients in a mixing glass filled with ice. Shake until chilled, about 15 seconds. Double strain into a chilled coupe. (No garnish.)

THE REAL DEAL

ERYN REECE, MAYAHUEL, NEW YORK CITY (2005)

Some cocktail names lie. They advertise promises that are broken within the glass. This name does not do that. Every ingredient here is the real deal and nothing but. Mayahuel put out a lot of great agave cocktails during its nine-year life. This is one of them, from a bartender who worked during the bar's early years. Reece was perhaps thinking simultaneously of the Manhattan and the Toronto, a cocktail that calls for whiskey and Fernet-Branca, when she came up with this burly and deep-flavored nightcap.

1½ ounces Sombra mezcal

¾ ounce Punt e Mes

¾ ounce Carpano Antica Formula vermouth

1 teaspoon Fernet-Branca

Combine the ingredients in a mixing glass three-quarters filled with ice. Stir until chilled, about 30 seconds. Strain into a chilled coupe. (No garnish.)

SFORZANDO

ERYN REECE, DEATH & CO, NEW YORK CITY (2012)

Rye, mezcal, and Bénédictine enjoy a subtly spicy *connaissance* in this drink, which impresses as a mezcal-based Perfect Manhattan of sorts. You'll get to the bottom of the glass and still not quite comprehend the drink's complex flavor profile. Best to make a second one to get to the bottom of it.

1 ounce Rittenhouse rye

¾ ounce Del Maguey Chichicapa mezcal

½ ounce Bénédictine

½ ounce Dolin dry vermouth

2 dashes Bittermens Xocolatl mole bitters

Orange twist for garnish

Combine the ingredients, except the garnish, in a mixing glass three-quarters filled with ice. Stir until chilled, about 30 seconds. Strain into a chilled coupe. Express the orange twist over the surface and drop it into the drink.

SINGLE VILLAGE FIX

THAD VOGLER, BERETTA, SAN FRANCISCO (2008)

This was one of the first drinks in the cocktail renaissance to use mezcal as a base. In its original version, Vogler used Del Maguey Chichicapa mezcal. His menu at Beretta was known for its inventive and varied use of sweeteners, in this case a pineapple gum syrup made by San Francisco outfit Small Hand Foods. That item can be found in specialty stores in many large cities, as well as online.

1½ ounces mezcal

¾ ounce freshly squeezed lime juice

¾ ounce Small Hand Foods pineapple gum syrup

Combine the ingredients in a cocktail shaker three-quarters filled with ice. Shake until chilled, about 15 seconds. Strain into a chilled coupe. (No garnish.)

SMOKE
AND ICE

JESSICA GONZALEZ, MARKET ST.,
RHINEBECK, NEW YORK (2016)

This mezcal Negroni variation is given a unique flavor through the pineapple infusion of the Campari, which sweetens the bitter liqueur; and the chocolate garnish. It is reminiscent of the Left Hand, a riff on the Boulevardier by bartender Sam Ross, which calls for chocolate bitters and tastes as candylike as this confection. For the chocolate, Gonzalez suggests dark chocolate at least 70 percent cacao.

1½ ounces mezcal

1 ounce Pineapple-Infused Campari (page 150)

1 ounce sweet vermouth

Dark chocolate for garnish

Combine the ingredients, except the garnish, in a mixing glass three-quarters filled with ice. Stir until chilled, about 30 seconds. Strain into a rocks glass over one large ice cube. Using a Microplane, garnish with three or four shavings of chocolate.

STRANGERS IN PARADISE

SHANNON MUSTIPHER, GLADY'S, NEW YORK (2016)

Strangers, indeed, as mezcal and rum rarely keep company in a cocktail. This is a creamy mezcal riff on a mai tai from tiki expert Shannon Mustipher, in which the various ingredients come together swimmingly. The Fernet float makes for an unusual and winning final touch. Orgeat Works makes a good macadamia orgeat that is available in some liquor stores and online. A lime shell—a traditional tiki garnish—is simply what's left of half a lime after you've squeezed the juice out of it.

1 ounce rhum agricole blanc

½ ounce aged rum

½ ounce mezcal espadín

½ ounce ginger liqueur

¾ ounce macadamia orgeat

¾ ounce freshly squeezed lime juice

⅛ ounce Fernet-Vallet liqueur

Lime shell for garnish

Mint sprig for garnish

Pineapple wedge for garnish

Combine all the ingredients, except the fernet and garnishes, in a cocktail shaker filled with ice. Shake until chilled, about 15 seconds. Strain into a chilled highball or tall tiki mug filled with pebble ice. Float the fernet on the surface of the drink. Top with more pebble ice. Garnish with the lime shell, mint sprig, and pineapple wedge.

SWEET MEZCAL MARTINI

ROBERT SIMONSON, BROOKLYN (2020)

In the martini's early years, from the 1880s until the advent of Prohibition in 1920, not all of them were dry. There were sweet martinis, made with Old Tom gin and sweet vermouth, and medium martinis, where the vermouth was half sweet and half dry. Some of these martini ancestors actually used more vermouth than gin. (And these drinks, while not recognizable to martini mavens of today, were, believe me, delicious.) I have applied those bygone standards to this recipe. The vermouth calms down the ferocious flavors of the mezcal, creating a drink so lovely and gentle, it is almost difficult to imagine that mezcal lurks inside its core. Sweet martinis were typically garnished with a cherry. That finishing touch works in this formulation as well.

2 ounces Dolin blanc vermouth

1 ounce mezcal

2 dashes orange bitters

Cherry for garnish

Combine the ingredients, except the garnish, in a mixing glass three-quarters filled with ice. Stir until chilled, about 30 seconds. Strain into a chilled coupe. Garnish with the cherry.

TEXICAN EGG NOG

DAVID WONDRICH

David Wondrich, cocktail historian and punch maker nonpareil, was the first person to tell me that mezcal made for a good eggnog. This is his version of the eggnog that the Texan prisoners of General Santa Anna put together with ingredients they bribed their guards to smuggle in order to celebrate San Jacinto Day (the Texas Republic's big independence holiday) on April 21, 1843. They used donkey's milk and didn't include chocolate, but according to Wondrich, the recipe is otherwise close to the original. One batch serves twenty.

4 cups unpasteurized cow's milk

One 2.7-ounce disk Mexican dark chocolate

10 jumbo eggs, separated

1¼ cups sugar, plus more as needed

¼ teaspoon ground cloves

½ teaspoon ground cinnamon

One 750-ml bottle mezcal, preferably Del Maguey Santo Domingo Albarradas

To a medium saucepan over low heat, add the milk. Grate the chocolate into the milk and cook, stirring, until the chocolate has dissolved. Do not let the milk boil. Let cool.

Separate the eggs. In a large nonreactive bowl (stainless-steel or ceramic), whip the egg whites with an electric mixer or a whisk until they form stiff peaks. In a separate 4-quart bowl, beat the egg yolks, sugar, and spices until creamy.

Stir the chocolate milk into the yolk mixture, and add the mezcal. Fold in the egg whites. Stir in more sugar if needed. Keep refrigerated until serving.

TÍA MIA

Though this drink made its debut at Lani Kai, a short-lived tiki bar in Manhattan, it secured its reputation at Leyenda, where it has been on the menu since the Brooklyn-based, Latin-spirits-focused cocktail bar opened in 2015. It is basically a mezcal mai tai—the clever name is an anagram—proving once again that mezcal is an improbably adaptable spirit and can find a home in nearly any classic cocktail formula. (If you don't have the pineapple frond and orchid on hand, don't sweat it—just drink the drink.)

1 ounce Del Maguey Vida mezcal

1 ounce Appleton Estate Reserve rum

½ ounce toasted almond orgeat, preferably Orgeat Works T'Orgeat

¼ ounce orange curaçao, preferably Pierre Ferrand

¾ ounce freshly squeezed lime juice

Lime wheel for garnish

Pineapple frond for garnish

Edible orchid for garnish

Combine the ingredients, except the garnishes, in a cocktail shaker filled with ice. Shake until chilled, about 15 seconds. Strain into a chilled double old-fashioned glass filled with crushed ice. Garnish with the lime wheel, pineapple frond, and edible orchid.

UNEXPECTED VICTORY

JAY SCHROEDER, *UNDERSTANDING MEZCAL* (2018)

Jay Schroeder has run the cocktail programs at several acclaimed restaurants and mezcalerias, and is the author of the excellent and unflinching agave primer *Understanding Mezcal* (2018). He points out, quite correctly, that gin and mezcal don't often find themselves in the same cocktail. "Maybe this one requires an asterisk," he says, "as the genever-style gin plays with the mezcal in a very different way than a London dry would. It's toasty, grainy, round, and subtle." For the coconut cream, if you can't find D'Best, an imported brand, any quality coconut cream (preferably frozen) will do the trick here. Some may require pulling back just a touch on the simple syrup. All the other elements here, added Schroeder, "are subversively dark—Angostura bitters, coffee liqueur, and toasted black sesame bring some sneaky bitter complexity into an otherwise breezy and tropical endeavor."

Crushed black sesame seeds to rim the glass

1 ounce Banhez Ensemble mezcal

½ ounce Bols genever

½ ounce all-natural coconut liqueur, preferably Kalani

¼ ounce coffee liqueur

¾ ounce freshly squeezed lime juice

¾ ounce simple syrup (1:1 sugar to water)

½ ounce D'Best fresh coconut cream

2 dashes Angostura bitters

Half-rim a ceramic cup with crushed black sesame seeds. Combine the remaining ingredients in a cocktail shaker filled with ice. Shake until chilled, about 15 seconds. Strain into the prepared cup. (No garnish.)

ZTINGER

ROBERT SIMONSON, BROOKLYN (2020)

Why does mezcal get along so beautifully with crème de menthe?
Do the herbaceous qualities of the spirit marry well with mint? Does
the smoke of the liquor find a perfect counterpoint in the sweetness
of the liqueur? Who can say? Enjoy your mezcal stinger!

2¼ ounces mezcal

¾ ounce Tempus Fugit
crème de menthe

Combine the ingredients in a mixing glass
three-quarters filled with ice. Stir until chilled,
about 30 seconds. Strain into a chilled coupe.
(No garnish.)

TEQUILA

COCKTAILS

THE ARMADA

LYNNETTE MARRERO, NEW YORK CITY (2010)

This is a reverse Negroni variation, created by Marreo, a prominent New York–based bartender and activist, to celebrate the 150th anniversary of Campari. Though the portion of bitter Campari has been increased, the mellowness of the soft, sweet cream sherry evens out the flavor, while the tequila plays the subtlest of roles. The recipe works with amontillado sherry, if you can't find cream sherry.

1½ ounces Campari
1 ounce Hidalgo cream sherry
¾ ounce tequila blanco
Grapefruit twist for garnish

Combine the ingredients, except the garnish, in a mixing glass three-quarters filled with ice. Stir until chilled, about 30 seconds. Strain into a chilled coupe. Express the grapefruit twist over the surface and drop it into the drink.

AUGIE MARCH

PHIL WARD, DEATH & CO, NEW YORK CITY (2008)

Sometime in the '00s, New York bartender Phil Ward came up with "Mr. Potato Head," a near foolproof method for inventing new cocktails. This cocktail is a fine example of that strategy. The basic idea is to subtract one ingredient from a cocktail formula that already works, and plug in something vaguely similar. For the most part, Ward practiced this method on old classics. In this case, however, he took on a modern classic, Audrey Saunders's Little Italy, created in 2005, which is basically a rye Manhattan with a bit of Cynar added. The Augie March is a tequila Manhattan with Cynar. The name comes from a Saul Bellow novel, *The Adventures of Augie March* (1953), whose hero has some misadventures in Mexico.

2 ounces El Tesoro
reposado tequila

¾ ounce Carpano Antica
Formula vermouth

½ ounce Cynar

Brandied cherry for garnish

Combine the ingredients, except the garnish, in a mixing glass three-quarters filled with ice. Stir until chilled, about 15 seconds. Strain into a chilled coupe. Garnish with the brandied cherry.

BENNY BLANCO

YANA VOLFSON, COSME, NEW YORK CITY (2016)

Yana Volfson, a master of agave cocktails, introduces a playful array of sweet, spicy, and bitter flavors—including Ancho Reyes, a poblano-chile-flavored liqueur from Mexico—to this spin on a Negroni. To make a horse's neck twist, you'll need a channel knife. Grip the orange firmly with one hand and, with your other hand, press the knife into the rind at the top of the fruit. Slowly and carefully work your way down and around the fruit's surface. Keep ¼ inch of space between the peels.

1 ounce blanco tequila, preferably Tapatio

½ ounce Aperol

½ ounce Campari

½ ounce bianco vermouth, preferably Carpano

½ ounce Ancho Reyes chile liqueur

Blood orange horse's neck twist for garnish

Combine the ingredients, except the garnish, in a mixing glass three-quarters filled with ice. Stir until chilled, about 15 seconds. Strain into a chilled rocks glass over one large ice cube. Garnish with the blood orange horse's neck twist.

CAMINANTE

JUSTIN LANE BRIGGS, CABINET, NEW YORK CITY (2019)

This simple yet singular cocktail was on the debut menu at Cabinet, a Manhattan bar dedicated to agave spirits and rye whiskey. With its unique combination of orgeat and Giffard Menthe-Pastille liqueur, the cocktail illustrates once again that agave spirits (in this case, jalapeño-infused tequila) can mix with almost anything. The interplay of the almond, hot pepper, and mint is endlessly beguiling. It's a near-perfect concoction, both surprising and seamless.

2 ounces Jalapeño-Infused
Azteca Azul Tequila Plata
(page 148)

¾ ounce Giffard orgeat

¾ ounce freshly squeezed
lemon juice

1 teaspoon Giffard
Menthe-Pastille

Combine the ingredients in a cocktail shaker filled with ice. Shake until chilled, about 15 seconds. Strain into a chilled coupe. (No garnish.)

DEATH FLIP

CHRIS HYSTED-ADAMS, BLACK PEARL,
MELBOURNE, AUSTRALIA (2010)

This intimidating-looking mélange has become a modern classic in Australia. Don't let the ingredient list scare you.

1 ounce blanco tequila

½ ounce yellow Chartreuse

½ ounce Jägermeister

Dash of simple syrup (1:1 sugar to water)

1 egg

Freshly ground nutmeg for garnish

Combine the ingredients, except the garnish, in a cocktail shaker filled with ice. Shake vigorously until chilled, about 15 seconds. Strain into a chilled coupe. Garnish with freshly ground nutmeg.

MARGHERITA
MARGARITA

MEGAN DESCHAINE, CHARLESTON,
SOUTH CAROLINA (2017)

This clever cocktail, created for a tequila cocktail competition, takes us to that wonderful land that lies between the margarita and Bloody Mary, delivering all the delights those famous cocktails promise in one package. "This cocktail's inspiration came innocently enough after a night of drinking with a few bartender buddies, and we were giggling over the most ridiculous drink ideas we could think of," said Deschaine. "I thought a pizza cocktail sounded pretty damned tasty." Be sure to use good local tomatoes with plenty of tang and taste—try the local farmers' market—and fresh basil leaves. Both contribute enormously to the fresh bouquet and flavor of the drink.

Salt and pepper
to rim the glass

1 ripe tomato, quartered

8 to 10 basil leaves

1½ ounces blanco tequila

¾ ounce freshly squeezed
lime juice

½ ounce honey syrup
(1:1 honey to water)

4 dashes Bittermens
Hellfire shrub

2 dashes Scrappy's
celery bitters

Skewered mozzarella ball
and basil leaf for garnish

Half-rim a chilled rocks glass with salt and pepper and add a large ice cube. Muddle the tomato quarters and basil in a cocktail shaker. Add the remaining ingredients, except the garnish, and fill with ice. Shake vigorously until chilled, about 15 seconds. Double strain over the ice into the prepared glass. Garnish with the skewered mozzarella ball and basil leaf.

PAN AM

BEN WALKER, VALKYRIE, TULSA, OKLAHOMA (2019)

Every time I feel like grumbling about eight-ingredient cocktails, something like the Pan Am comes along. The spirit base is made up of tequila, anise-infused cachaça, and Giffard crème de pamplemousse. To this mixture are added lime juice, ginger syrup, and dashes of absinthe, green Chartreuse, and salt solution. The unexpectedly unified result comes off like a creamy, herbal margarita served on crushed ice, and goes down like a soothing scoop of boozy anise ice cream.

1 ounce Agavales
blanco tequila

½ ounce Anise-Infused
Leblon Cachaça (page 143)

½ ounce Giffard
crème de pamplemousse

½ ounce freshly squeezed
lime juice

⅓ ounce Ginger Syrup
(page 144)

Dash of Lucid absinthe

2 dashes green Chartreuse

2 drops Salt Solution
(page 151)

Combine the ingredients in a cocktail shaker filled with ice. Shake until chilled, about 15 seconds. Strain into a double old-fashioned glass over crushed ice. (No garnish.)

PIÑA VERDE

RYAN FITZGERALD, TODD SMITH,
AND ERICK REICHBORN–KJENNERUD,
ABV, SAN FRANCISCO (2014)

This drink—which began as an homage to another San Francisco cocktail, the modern classic Chartreuse Swizzle—is aptly named. It tastes a bit like a slightly unripe pineapple, in a good way. The lime and pineapple elements are perfectly balanced, but it's the génépy, an herbal liqueur from the Alpine region of Europe, that sets the drink apart and makes it more than simply a variation on a pineapple margarita. It lends the drink its bright, tangy, airy quality, and makes it a perfect cocktail for summertime day drinking. Ryan Fitzgerald, an owner of ABV, strongly recommends Tapatio, an excellent tequila.

2 ounces highland blanco tequila, preferably Tapatio

¾ ounce Dolin Génépy des Alpes liqueur

1 ounce freshly squeezed lime juice

¾ ounce Small Hand Foods pineapple gum syrup

4 dashes orange bitters

Pineapple wedge for garnish

Combine the ingredients, except the garnish, in a cocktail shaker filled with ice. Shake until chilled, about 15 seconds. Strain into a chilled coupe. Garnish with the pineapple wedge.

RED GRASSHOPPER

MICHAEL MADRUSAN, THE EVERLEIGH,
MELBOURNE, AUSTRALIA (2011)

Michael Madrusan is a veteran of the late Sasha Petraske's cocktail bar empire, and that influence shows in this drink. He keeps it simple, as was Petraske's way. It is basically a tequila daiquiri made with a rich honey syrup, instead of sugar, and the rich honey syrup—three parts honey to one part water—is straight from the Petraske handbook. The unusual garnish of smoked paprika not only lends a nice bite to each sip, but also provides a lovely visual contrast to the light green drink. (The paprika also contributes enough smoky flavor that you might mistake the tequila used here for mezcal.)

2 ounces tequila

1 ounce freshly squeezed lime juice

¾ ounce rich honey syrup (3:1 honey to water)

Smoked paprika for garnish

Combine the ingredients, except the garnish, in a cocktail shaker filled with ice. Shake until chilled, about 15 seconds. Strain into a chilled coupe. Garnish the surface of the drink with a light dusting of smoked paprika.

ROSALITA

DYLAN O'BRIEN, PRIZEFIGHTER,
EMERYVILLE, CALIFORNIA (2015)

Bartender Dylan O'Brien is the brain behind Mezcal Monday, a weekly happening at Prizefighter, a wonderfully unpretentious cocktail bar in the San Francisco Bay Area community of Emeryville. He describes this drink as "essentially a Tommy's Margarita with the addition of amaro." And that, thankfully, is what it is. The ½ ounce of Amaro Montenegro, from Bologna, Italy, adds some welcome baking-spice bottom notes to the cocktail. The drink is named after a song by Bruce Springsteen.

Kosher salt to rim the glass

2 ounces reposado tequila

½ ounce Amaro Montenegro

¾ ounce freshly squeezed lime juice

¾ ounce agave syrup (1:1 agave nectar to water)

Half-rim a chilled rocks glass with salt and fill with a few large ice cubes. Combine the remaining ingredients in a cocktail shaker filled with ice. Shake until chilled, about 15 seconds. Strain over the ice into the prepared rocks glass. (No garnish.)

SEAN AND JUAN

BRAD SMITH, LATITUDE 29, NEW ORLEANS (2019)

You don't see many agave-based tiki drinks. But proponents of the neotiki movement of the last decade have been more adventurous, reaching for bottles previously considered beyond tikidom's tight circle of rums, juices, and exotic liqueurs. I encountered this easygoing sipper at Latitude 29, the tiki bar founded by modern-day tiki poo-bah Jeff "Beachbum" Berry. If the presence of tequila in a tiki drink hadn't been enough to draw my attention, the odd-couple pairing of tequila and Jameson blended Irish whiskey would've clinched it. An odd split spirit base indeed, but the guava and crème de cacao safely tug the drink back to the tropics. (Berry actually had the name for the drink, after the two main characters in his favorite Sergio Leone Western, and the concept, Irish whiskey and tequila, before bartender Brad Smith came up with the liquid answer to his challenge.)

1 ounce tequila

½ ounce Jameson Irish whiskey

¾ ounce crème de cacao

1 teaspoon Bénédictine

½ ounce freshly squeezed lemon juice

½ ounce simple syrup (1:1 sugar to water)

½ ounce guava puree

1 teaspoon Bénédictine

½ lemon wheel for garnish

Combine the ingredients, except the garnish, in a cocktail shaker half-filled with ice. Shake until chilled, about 15 seconds. Strain into a double old-fashioned glass over two large ice cubes. Garnish with the half lemon wheel.

SIESTA

KATIE STIPE, FLATIRON LOUNGE,
NEW YORK CITY (2006)

You can't have a conversation about modern tequila cocktails without talking about the Siesta, a spicy, bitter spin on a Hemingway Daiquiri from the young days of the modern cocktail revival. Katie Stipe, one of the early figures in the cocktail renaissance in New York, invented it at the Flatiron Lounge, an influential and formative cocktail bar in Manhattan that operated from 2003 to 2018.

1½ ounces blanco tequila

¼ ounce Campari

¾ ounce freshly squeezed lime juice

½ ounce freshly squeezed grapefruit juice

¾ ounce simple syrup (1:1 sugar to water)

Lime wheel for garnish

Combine the ingredients, except the garnish, in a cocktail shaker three-quarters filled with ice. Shake until chilled, about 15 seconds. Strain into a chilled coupe. Garnish with the lime wheel.

SPICY PALOMA

PHIL WARD, MAYAHUEL, NEW YORK CITY (2009)

Phil Ward served tons of palomas at Mayahuel during the bar's nine-year existence. This simple tequila highball is usually made with carbonated grapefruit soda, often Squirt. Ward prefers fresh grapefruit juice to lend the drink genuine grapefruit flavor, while the Jarritos club soda gives the drink the expected effervescence. The jalapeño infusion contributes a kick to a drink that can otherwise come off as a little dull. Ward says the infusion takes the drink to "a new whole level."

Salt to rim the glass

2 ounces Jalapeño-Infused Blanco Tequila (page 149)

1 ounce freshly squeezed grapefruit juice

¾ ounce freshly squeezed lime juice

½ ounce agave syrup (1:1 agave nectar to water)

Jarritos club soda to top

Lime wedge for garnish

Half-rim a chilled highball glass with salt and fill with a few large ice cubes. Combine the remaining ingredients, except the club soda and garnish, in a cocktail shaker filled with ice. Shake until chilled, about 15 seconds. Strain over the ice into the prepared highball glass. Top with club soda, and garnish with the lime wedge.

TEQUILA
AND TONIC

IVY MIX, LEYENDA, BROOKLYN

Gin doesn't own tonic water. The mixer is combined with a variety of spirits the world over, from rum to white port to Calvados. Ivy Mix, an owner of Leyenda, a Brooklyn bar with a focus on Latin spirits, thinks this drink requires an earthy lowlands tequila, such as Partida reposado, which is aged slightly and has toasty, nutty flavors. "Just as you want a really gin-y gin, I want a really tequila-y tequila," said Mix. For the tonic, she reaches for Canada Dry or Schweppes, which have "more quinine kick" in her opinion. For a twist, try this recipe with mezcal. But since that smoky spirit typically has a more pungent flavor, use only 1½ ounces.

Lime wedge

2 ounces tequila, preferably Partida reposado

4 ounces tonic water, preferably Canada Dry or Schweppes

Fill a chilled highball glass with ice. Squeeze the lime over the ice and drop it in the glass. Add the tequila and top with the tonic water. Stir briefly. (No garnish.)

TOMMY'S MARGARITA

JULIO BERMEJO, TOMMY'S MEXICAN RESTAURANT,
SAN FRANCISCO (EARLY 1990S)

Julio Bermejo inherited the bar at his family's Mexican restaurant in the 1980s. Soon after, he took an interest in the bottles behind that bar and dedicated himself to bringing better tequila—and a better understanding of tequila—to his customers. His simple yet essential hack on the traditional margarita was to eighty-six the Cointreau, switch out the sugar for agave syrup, and use only quality 100-percent-agave tequila. Thus, what came to be known as Tommy's Margarita was born. (It did not bear that name when it was created in the 1990s; it was simply the house margarita.) These may all seem like common-sense adjustments to us today, but they were revolutionary at the time. Bermejo made the alterations to draw attention to the flavor of the spirit itself. Some argue that the name is a misnomer, because without the orange liqueur, this is not a margarita at all. No one argues, however, that it's not delicious.

Salt to rim the glass

2 ounces reposado tequila

1 ounce freshly squeezed lime juice

½ ounce agave syrup (1:1 agave nectar to water)

Lime wedge for garnish

Half-rim a chilled rocks glass with salt and fill with ice. Combine the remaining ingredients, except the garnish, in a cocktail shaker filled with ice. Shake until chilled, about 15 seconds. Strain into the prepared glass. Garnish with the lime wedge.

UNDER THE VOLCANO

KYLE DAVIDSON, *BETA COCKTAILS* (2011)

There's something about Malcolm Lowry's novel *Under the Volcano* (1947) that inspires agave cocktails. There's Firmin's Folly (page 38), in the Mezcal Cocktails chapter, and then there's this earlier drink, a variation on the Last Word, that first appeared in the influential *Beta Cocktails* (2011) by Maks Pazuniak and Kirk Estopinal.

2 ounces El Tesoro añejo tequila

Scant ¼ ounce yellow Chartreuse

Scant ½ ounce Cynar

¾ ounce freshly squeezed lime juice

¼ ounce agave nectar

Combine the ingredients in a cocktail shaker filled with ice. Shake until chilled, about 15 seconds. Strain into a chilled coupe. (No garnish.)

MEZCAL + TEQUILA

COCKTAILS

CAMARÓN COCKTAIL

ROBERT SIMONSON, BROOKLYN (2019)

The Cameron's Kick, a 1920s drink of uncertain origin, is one of my favorite unsung cocktails. Some crazy bartender decided that mixing Scotch, Irish whiskey, and orgeat might be a good idea, and I'm very grateful that they did. Knowing how well tequila and mezcal play together in many of the modern agave cocktails I enjoy, I thought perhaps they might perform well in this drink. Indeed, they did. The tequila steps in for the Irish whiskey and the smoky mezcal for the equally smoky Scotch. Sometimes the simplest ideas work best. It is named for a battle between the Mexican army and the French Foreign Legion in 1863.

1 ounce tequila

1 ounce mezcal

¾ ounce freshly squeezed lemon juice

½ ounce orgeat

Combine the ingredients in a cocktail shaker filled with ice. Shake until chilled, about 15 seconds. Strain into a chilled coupe. (No garnish.)

HOT LIPS

JESSICA GONZALEZ, DEATH & CO,
NEW YORK CITY (2009)

Jessica Gonzalez came up with this early tequila-mezcal winner while bartending at Death & Co, in Manhattan. She took it with her when she moved to the chic bar at the NoMad Hotel twenty blocks uptown, where it became one of the bar's most popular orders. The cocktail is unusual because although it contains citrus, it is nonetheless stirred. The result is tart, sweet, piquant, and succulent all at the same time.

Salt to rim the glass

¾ ounce Jalapeño-Infused Blanco Tequila (page 149)

¾ ounce mezcal

½ ounce pineapple juice

½ ounce freshly squeezed lemon juice

½ ounce Vanilla Syrup (page 151)

1 teaspoon cane syrup

Half-rim a chilled rocks glass with salt and add a large ice cube. Combine the remaining ingredients in a mixing glass three-quarters filled with ice. Stir until chilled, about 30 seconds. Strain over the ice into the prepared glass. (No garnish.)

LIVING LA VIDA

MIMI BURNHAM, BAR CELONA,
NEW YORK CITY (2019)

The saffron syrup lends a vaguely exotic and rich air to this tart, bright, ever-so-slightly bitter cooler. And though the strands of saffron called for seem few, the flavor definitely comes through. The saffron also lends the drink an appealing yellow tint, enhanced by the amaro and lemon juice. You'll note that Mimi Burnham does not say to strain the saffron out of the syrup. "I like that I sometimes see a thread or two dancing in the highball because of the bubbles," she said.

1 ounce mezcal

¼ ounce blanco tequila

¾ ounce Amaro Montenegro

½ ounce freshly squeezed lemon juice

½ ounce Saffron Syrup (page 150)

2 ounces tonic water, preferably Fever-Tree Indian tonic

Lemon wheel for garnish

Combine the ingredients, except the tonic water and garnish, in a cocktail shaker three-quarters filled with ice. Shake until chilled, about 15 seconds. Strain into an ice-filled highball glass and top with the tonic water. Garnish with the lemon wheel.

LOS ALTOS

DAVE MOLYNEUX, THE EVERLEIGH,
MELBOURNE, AUSTRALIA (2017)

This simple highball aptly illustrates the flavor friendship agave spirits enjoy with lime and pineapple juice.

1½ ounces tequila

½ ounce mezcal

1½ ounces pineapple juice

½ ounce freshly squeezed lime juice

½ ounce simple syrup (1:1 sugar to water)

Soda water to top

2 pineapple leaves for garnish (optional)

Combine the ingredients, except the soda water and garnish, in a cocktail shaker filled with ice. Shake until chilled, about 15 seconds. Strain into a chilled collins glass filled with ice. Top with soda water, and garnish with the pineapple leaves, if you have them.

MEZCAL SUN-RISA

IGNACIO "NACHO" JIMENEZ, GHOST DONKEY,
NEW YORK CITY (2017)

Ignacio Jimenez, the former head bartender at Ghost Donkey, a popular agave bar in New York's East Village, devised this drink. His goal was to create a respectable mezcal answer to the tequila sunrise, a cocktail that has never quite overcome its trashy 1970s reputation as the Rolling Stones' favorite touring tipple. In addition to the mezcal, the hibiscus-habanero syrup steps in for the usual, and usually too sweet, grenadine. The bitter orange juice gives the drink a spine, which regular orange juice could never duplicate.

1 ounce tequila

1 ounce mezcal

4 ounces bitter orange juice, such as Goya

2 ounces freshly squeezed orange juice

¾ ounce Hibiscus-Habanero Syrup (page 146)

Dehydrated lemon wheel for garnish

Combine the ingredients, except the garnish, in a collins glass filled with ice. Briefly stir, about 5 seconds, to integrate and chill the ingredients. Carefully float the hibiscus-habanero syrup on the surface of the drink. Garnish with the dehydrated lemon wheel.

MORNING CALL

ALBA HUERTA, JULEP, HOUSTON (2015)

Here's a relatively simple agave collins crossed with a tequila and tonic. The critical and enchanting difference to this highball is the hibiscus-infused tonic water, which introduces a lovely hue and a subtle flavor note.

1½ ounces blanco tequila, preferably Ocho

2 barspoons mezcal

½ ounce freshly squeezed lime juice

½ ounce agave nectar

About 2 ounces Hibiscus Tonic Water (page 148) to top

Lime wheel for garnish

Hibiscus flower for garnish (optional)

Combine the ingredients, except the tonic water and garnishes, in a cocktail shaker three-quarters filled with ice. Shake until chilled, about 15 seconds. Strain into a collins glass filled with ice, and top with the tonic water. Garnish with the lime wheel and, if you can find one, the hibiscus flower.

OAXACA
OLD–FASHIONED

PHIL WARD, DEATH & CO, NEW YORK CITY (2007)

One of the first mezcal cocktails of the modern era, one of the most famous, and one of the easiest. Phil Ward's long love affair with agave spirits—as well as those of many of his customers, first at Death & Co, and later at his own bar, Mayahuel—began with this drink.

1½ ounces El Tesoro reposado tequila

½ ounce Del Maguey Chichicapa or San Luis Del Rio mezcal

1 barspoon agave syrup (1:1 agave nectar to water)

2 dashes Angostura bitters

1 piece orange zest, about the size of a silver dollar

Combine the ingredients, except the orange zest, in a chilled rocks glass with one large ice cube. Stir until chilled, about 30 seconds. Hold the orange zest, skin-side down, several inches above the drink. Light a match and use it to warm the skin side of the peel. Quickly squeeze the zest in the direction of the match. The oil from the zest will briefly burst into flame, showering its essence over the drink's surface.

QUICK STEP

NATASHA DAVID, NITECAP, NEW YORK CITY (2015)

There's only a teaspoon of peach liqueur in this light and lovely sipper, but does it ever come through. The blanc vermouth further mellows the effect. The mezcal and jalapeño-infused tequila combine to give that fruity flavor profile a gently biting backbone. At the time this drink was created, "there was an influx of smoky-peach cocktails, but all were shaken with citrus," David recalled. "I wanted to show that mezcal could be used in an 'elegant' martini-style cocktail. It's one of the drinks that still gets called for on the regular at Nitecap."

1½ ounces mezcal, preferably Del Maguey Vida

1 ounce Dolin blanc vermouth

½ ounce Jalapeño-Infused Blanco Tequila (page 149), preferably made with Pueblo Viejo

1 teaspoon Giffard crème de pêche

Combine the ingredients in a mixing glass three-quarters filled with ice. Stir until chilled, about 30 seconds. Strain into a chilled coupe. (No garnish.)

SALT AND ASH

MAKS PAZUNIAK, THE COUNTING ROOM,
BROOKLYN (2010)

A standout drink during Maks Pazuniak's short but memorable reign at the Counting Room in Brooklyn. Various layers of citrus, smoke, and sweet lead to a fascinating complexity. It is important to use the brands specified. The recipe looks complicated, and it does take a bit of prep time. But all the ingredients, except the lemon juice, can be combined ahead of time. Batch up a round of ten or twenty to save yourself some future labor. Trust me, you won't grow tired of drinking this cocktail.

¾ ounce Del Maguey
Chichicapa mezcal

¾ ounce Grapefruit-Infused
El Jimador Blanco Tequila
(page 145)

½ ounce Lapsang Souchong–
Infused Cinzano Sweet
Vermouth (page 149)

¼ ounce maraschino liqueur

½ ounce freshly squeezed
lemon juice

¼ ounce agave syrup
(1:1 agave nectar to water)

Dash of Angostura bitters

Dash of Regans'
orange bitters

Grapefruit twist for garnish

Combine the ingredients, except the garnish, in a mixing glass three-quarters filled with ice. Stir until chilled, about 30 seconds. Strain into a rocks glass over one large ice cube. Express the grapefruit twist over the drink and discard.

SPAGHETTI WESTERN

JESSICA GONZALEZ, DEATH & CO,
NEW YORK CITY (2011)

This sipping cocktail is not too far removed from the Oaxaca Old-Fashioned (page 136), a tequila-mezcal old-fashioned variation that was also created at Death & Co. Gonzalez's contribution was to add a dose of Amaro Nonino, a light, orangey Italian liqueur—and the "spaghetti" in this Western—which blends seamlessly with the other ingredients.

1 ounce reposado tequila, preferably Siete Leguas

½ ounce mezcal, preferably Los Nahuales

¾ ounce Amaro Nonino

Dash of orange bitters

Grapefruit twist for garnish

Combine the ingredients, except the garnish, in a mixing glass three-quarters filled with ice. Stir until chilled, about 30 seconds. Strain into chilled old-fashioned glass over one large ice cube. Express the grapefruit twist over the surface and drop it into the drink.

ANGELICA TINCTURE

2 ounces dried angelica root

16 ounces neutral overproof spirit, such as Everclear

Combine the angelica root and spirit in a glass jar. Set aside to infuse for 2 weeks. Strain into a clean jar and cover. The tincture will keep indefinitely at room temperature.

MAKES 2 CUPS

ANISE–INFUSED LEBLON CACHAÇA

1 liter Leblon cachaça

20 grams star anise

Combine the Leblon cachaça and star anise in a nonreactive (preferably glass) container and allow to infuse for 24 hours. Strain out the star anise and rebottle. The infusion will keep indefinitely at room temperature.

MAKES 1 LITER

CINNAMON SYRUP

2 cinnamon sticks

1 ounce gentian root

2 cups sugar

1 cup water

Break the cinnamon sticks into pieces. In a small pot over a low heat, toast the cinnamon until fragrant. Add the gentian, sugar, and water. Simmer until the sugar has dissolved. Remove from the heat and let cool. Strain into a jar, cover, and refrigerate for up to 1 week.

MAKES ABOUT 1 CUP

GINGER SYRUP

1 cup strained ginger juice (from an extractor)

1 cup water

2 cups cane sugar

In a small pot over low heat, combine the ingredients and cook, stirring, until the sugar is dissolved. Let cool to room temperature and refrigerate for up to 1 week. Note: If you haven't access to an extractor, Pratt Standard and Liber & Co. make good ginger syrups that are commercially available.

MAKES ABOUT 2 CUPS

GINGER WORT

3 cups water

8 ounces minced ginger

1½ ounces light brown sugar

¾ ounce freshly squeezed lime juice

In a small saucepan over medium heat, bring the water to a boil, pour into a nonreactive container, and add the ginger and brown sugar. Cover and set aside for 1½ hours. Strain through a chinois into a pitcher or bowl, pressing the ginger to extract as much liquid as possible. Stir in the lime juice. Transfer to a bottle or jar, cover, and refrigerate for up to 1 week.

MAKES ABOUT 3 CUPS

GRAPEFRUIT–INFUSED EL JIMADOR BLANCO TEQUILA

1 cup El Jimador Tequila

Peel of 1 large grapefruit

Combine the tequila and grapefruit peel in a nonreactive (preferably glass) container and allow to infuse for 24 hours. Strain out the peel, and rebottle. The infusion will keep indefinitely at room temperature.

MAKES ABOUT 1 CUP

HIBISCUS GRENADINE

1 cup pomegranate juice,
such as POM

6 grams dried hibiscus

1 cup sugar

In a small saucepan with a lid over medium heat, bring the pomegranate juice to a boil. Remove from the heat and add the hibiscus. Cover and steep for 7 minutes. Add the sugar and stir until dissolved. Strain through a fine-mesh strainer into a jar and store in the refrigerator for up to 1 week.

MAKES ABOUT 1 CUP

HIBISCUS–HABANERO SYRUP

400 grams sugar

14 ounces water

60 grams dried
hibiscus flowers

50 grams habanero pepper,
sliced

1 vanilla bean

5 orange twists

In a saucepan over medium-high heat, combine the sugar and water. Add the hibiscus flowers, habanero, vanilla bean, and orange twists. Bring the mixture to a boil, then remove from the heat. Allow to cool, strain into a clean container with a lid, and store in the refrigerator for up to 1 week.

MAKES ABOUT 1 CUP

HIBISCUS TONIC WATER

½ cup dried hibiscus flowers

1 liter tonic water, such as Fever Tree

Place the hibiscus flowers in a bowl. Pour the tonic water over the flowers and allow to infuse for 20 minutes. Strain. To retain carbonation, strain into a 1-liter soda siphon. Use immediately.

MAKES 1 LITER

JALAPEÑO-INFUSED AZTECA AZUL TEQUILA PLATA

1 to 2 jalapeño peppers, sliced into ¼-inch wheels

1 liter tequila

Combine the peppers and tequila in a non-reactive (preferably glass) container and allow to infuse for 18 to 24 hours. Sample the infusion periodically after the 18-hour mark; be careful not to overinfuse! It will become too hot and bitter. At the desired heat and flavor balance, strain out all solids from the tequila and rebottle. The infusion will keep indefinitely at room temperature.

MAKES 1 LITER

JALAPEÑO-INFUSED BLANCO TEQUILA

One 750-ml bottle blanco tequila

½ jalapeño pepper, chopped

Combine the tequila with the pepper in a nonreactive (preferably glass) container and allow to infuse for 20 minutes, tasting frequently to make sure the heat level is to your liking. Strain out the pepper, transfer to a clean bottle, and seal. The infusion will keep indefinitely at room temperature.

MAKES 750 MILLILITERS

LAPSANG SOUCHONG— INFUSED CINZANO SWEET VERMOUTH

12½ ounces Cinzano sweet vermouth

¾ cup loose Lapsang souchong tea

Combine the vermouth and tea in a nonreactive (preferably glass) container and allow to infuse for 4 to 6 hours. Strain out the tea, transfer the vermouth to a clean bottle, and seal. The infusion will keep for up to 1 week at room temperature.

MAKES 12½ OUNCES

PINEAPPLE–INFUSED CAMPARI

1 cup fresh pineapple, cut into small chunks

8 ounces Campari

In a bowl, stir together the pineapple and Campari. Transfer to a jar, seal the lid, and let infuse for 36 hours, agitating the jar three times while the Campari is infusing. Fine strain into a clean jar, discard the pineapple, and seal. The tincture will keep in the refrigerator for up to 1 month.

MAKES ABOUT 1 CUP

SAFFRON SYRUP

1 cup water

1 cup sugar

4 long or 8 short saffron strands

In a small saucepan over medium heat, bring the water to a boil. Add the sugar and stir to dissolve. Remove the pan from the heat, add the saffron threads, and stir to incorporate. Allow to cool and then transfer to a container with a lid. The syrup will keep for up to 6 months at room temperature.

MAKES ABOUT 1 CUP

SALT SOLUTION

3½ ounces water
½ ounce kosher salt

Combine the ingredients and stir until dissolved. Use immediately.

MAKES 3½ OUNCES

SPICED DEMERARA SYRUP

4 cinnamon sticks
5 whole cloves
2 whole star anise
1 cup water
2 cups demerara sugar

Break the cinnamon sticks into large pieces. In a small saucepan over low heat, lightly toast the spices. Add the water and sugar (water first, or the sugar will burn). Simmer on medium-low heat until the sugar is completely dissolved. Pour the syrup into a container, cover, and refrigerate overnight. Strain the syrup into a jar and cover. Store in the refrigerator for up to 1 week.

MAKES ABOUT 1 CUP

VANILLA SYRUP

1 cup water
1 cup sugar
1 vanilla bean, split

In a small saucepan over low heat, combine the water and sugar. Simmer until the sugar dissolves. Add the vanilla bean to the mixture. Continue simmering for 4 minutes. Remove from the heat and let cool. Strain through a cheesecloth-lined sieve into a clean container and cover. The syrup will keep in the refrigerator for up to 1 week.

MAKES ABOUT 1 CUP

COCKTAIL REFERENCE GUIDE

Mezcal and tequila function in almost every cocktail format that exists. So if you have a favorite cocktail, there's a very good chance there's an agave equivalent for it in this book. The following handy guide will help you find it.

IF YOUR
DRINK IS A

BLOODY MARY

TRY

Margherita
Margarita ◆ 104

IF YOUR
DRINK IS A

DAIQUIRI

TRY

Mezcal Fix ◆ 58

Mezcal Sour ◆ 64

Red Grasshopper ◆ 109

Siesta ◆ 114

Single Village
Fix ◆ 79

IF YOUR
DRINK IS A

MAI TAI

TRY

Caminante ◆ 100

Tía Mia ◆ 87

IF YOUR DRINK IS A

MANHATTAN

TRY

Augie March ◆ 96

Elegante ◆ 37

Mezcal Cocktail ◆ 49

Mezcaletti ◆ 55

Sforzando ◆ 77

IF YOUR DRINK IS A

MARGARITA

TRY

Gun Metal Blue ◆ 41

Mezcal Margarita ◆ 59

Rosalita ◆ 110

IF YOUR DRINK IS A

MARTINI

TRY

Firmin's Folly ◆ 38

Martina ◆ 46

Sweet Mezcal Martini ◆ 85

IF YOUR DRINK IS A

MOSCOW MULE

TRY

Mezcal Mule ◆ 61

IF YOUR DRINK IS A

NEGRONI

TRY

The Armada ◆ 95

Benny Blanco ◆ 99

The Last Mechanical Art ◆ 45

Mezcalero ◆ 65

Mezcal Negroni ◆ 62

The Real Deal ◆ 74

Smoke and Ice ◆ 80

IF YOUR DRINK IS AN

OLD-FASHIONED

TRY

Oaxaca Old-Fashioned ◆ 136

Spaghetti Western ◆ 141

IF YOUR
DRINK IS A

STINGER OR ALEXANDER

TRY

Cocoa Smoke ◆ 33

Mezcalexander ◆ 57

Polar Bear ◆ 73

Ztinger ◆ 91

IF YOUR
DRINK IS A

TOM COLLINS

TRY

Living la Vida ◆ 129

Los Altos ◆ 130

Mezcal Collins ◆ 51

IF YOUR
DRINK IS A

WHISKEY SOUR

TRY

Camarón Cocktail ◆ 125

Hot Lips ◆ 126

Mezcal Fix ◆ 58

Mezcal Sour ◆ 64

 **BIBLIOGRAPHY**

If, while making and enjoying these drinks, you become curious to find out more about the history, tradition, practices, politics, and economics of mezcal and tequila, a few books have come out in recent years that can fill you in. Some recommended volumes are listed below.

Cooper, Ron, and Chantal Martineau. *Finding Mezcal.* California and New York: Ten Speed Press, 2018.

Janzen, Emma. *Mezcal: The History, Craft and Cocktails of the World's Ultimate Artisanal Spirit.* McGregor, MN: Voyageur Press, 2017.

Martineau, Chantal. *How the Gringos Stole Tequila: The Modern Age of Mexico's Most Traditional Spirit.* Chicago: Chicago Review Press, 2015.

Schroeder, James. *Understanding Mezcal.* Chicago and Mexico City: Prensa Press, 2018.

ACKNOWLEDGMENTS

I'd like to thank the following bartenders and sundry liquor pros for their contributions to this book, both big and small: M. Carrie Allan, Julio Bermejo, Jeff Berry, Richard Boccato, Justin Lane Briggs, Mony Bunni, Mimi Burnham, Charles Cerankosky, Ron Cooper, Gary Crunkleton, Laura Cullen, Natasha David, Alex Day, Megan Deschaine, Ryan Fitzgerald, Jenna Gerbino, Jessica Gonzalez, Josh Harris, Scott Henkle, Alba Huerta, Chris Hysted-Adams, Ignacio Jimenez, Misty Kalkofen, Caitlin Laman, Michael Madrusan, Lynnette Marrero, Franky Marshall, Jim Meehan, Matteo Meletti, Janet Mick, Ivy Mix, Dave Molyneux, Shannon Mustipher, Dylan O'Brien, Steve Olson, Josie Packard, Maks Pazuniak, Aaron Post, Eryn Reece, Jon Santer, James Schroeder, Joaquín Simó, Brad Smith, Katie Stipe, Arik Torren, Thad Vogler, Yana Volfson, Ben Walker, Phil Ward, Ellie Winters, David Wondrich, and Marco Zappia. Special thanks to our vastly talented drink stylists, Fanny Chu and Dan Greenbaum, who helped make the cocktails look as dazzling as they do. Also, tremendous thanks to my peerless collaborator in cocktail apps, Martin Doudoroff.

Gratitude and heartfelt thanks to my agent, David Black, who does everything a literary agent should do, and does it exceedingly well. And to Aaron Wehner, Ashley Pierce, Julie Bennett, Betsy Stromberg, Allison Renzulli, David Hawk, and all the folks at Ten Speed Press and Penguin Random House who are so skilled at taking my work and transforming it into beautiful books. Additional thanks to Lizzie Munro, one of the best and most intuitive cocktail photographers in the business.

Finally, endless love and gratitude to my wife Mary Kate, my son Asher, and my stepson Richard.

ABOUT THE AUTHOR

ROBERT SIMONSON writes about cocktails for a living. Yes, in answer to the question he fields almost daily, that's a real job. He is the author of *The Old-Fashioned* (2014), *A Proper Drink* (2016), *3-Ingredient Cocktails* (2017), and *The Martini Cocktail* (2019). *3-Ingredient Cocktails* and *The Martini Cocktail* were nominated for James Beard Awards. In 2019, he won a Spirited Award for Best Cocktail Writer, which seemed merciful since he had lost the previous ten times. He has for twenty years written for a dozen different departments of the *New York Times,* most frequently the Food, Travel, and Arts sections. He also writes for other food and drink publications with titles that sound like they should be followed by an exclamation point: *Imbibe, Punch, Grub Street.* He's created two apps in collaboration with Martin Doudoroff, "Modern Classics for the Cocktail Renaissance" and "The Martini Cocktail," which you should consider buying. No, really, you should. They're very good. Promise. His social media presence has dwindled over the years until all that he can cope with anymore is Instagram. He successfully raised a son and sent him to college on a freelancer's income. He has a wonderful wife, Mary Kate, who steers him away from his worst story ideas. He's from Milwaukee but has lived in Brooklyn for what seems like forever. He dreams of opening a bar, but probably never will. Favorite drink: old-fashioned. Second favorite: martini. Third favorite: seltzer. A hot dog is a sandwich. Chicago deep-dish is pizza. "More than," not "over." Fight me.

INDEX

Published in the United States by Ten Speed Press, an imprint of
Random House, a division of Penguin Random House LLC, New York.
www.tenspeed.com

Ten Speed Press and the Ten Speed Press colophon are registered
trademarks of Penguin Random House LLC.

Library of Congress Cataloging-in-Publication Data
  Names: Simonson, Robert, author.
  Title: Mezcal and tequila cocktails : mixed drinks for the golden
    age of agave / by Robert Simonson.
  Description: First edition. | California : Ten Speed Press, [2021] |
    Includes bibliographical references and index.
  Identifiers: LCCN 2020014445 (print) | LCCN 2020014446 (ebook) |
    ISBN 9781984857743 (hardcover) | ISBN 9781984857750 (ebook)
  Subjects: LCSH: Tequila. | Mescal. | Cooking (Fructose) | Tequila—History. |
    Mescal—History. | LCGFT: Cookbooks.
  Classification: LCC TP607.T46 S56 2021 (print) | LCC TP607.T46 (ebook) |
    DDC 641.8/74—dc23
  LC record available at https://lccn.loc.gov/2020014445
  LC ebook record available at https://lccn.loc.gov/2020014446

Hardcover ISBN: 978-1-9848-5774-3
eBook ISBN: 978-1-9848-5775-0

Printed in China

Acquiring editor: Julie Bennett | Project editor: Ashley Pierce
Art director and designer: Betsy Stromberg | Production designer: Mari Gill
Production manager: Dan Myers | Prepress color manager: Jane Chinn
Drink stylists: Fanny Chu and Dan Greenbaum | Prop stylist: Lizzie Munro
Copyeditor: Deborah Kops | Proofreader: Emily Timberlake
Indexer: Ken DellaPenta
Publicist: David Hawk | Marketer: Chloe Aryeh

10 9 8 7 6 5 4 3 2 1

First Edition